# everyday GoodFood
## Stir-fries &
## quick fixes

Editor **Sharon Brown**

BOOKS

# Contents

# Introduction

Even though we all lead such busy lives these days, it's not difficult to prepare delicious home-cooked meals – if you've got the right recipes to hand.

Whether it's a weeknight supper, light lunch or casual supper for friends or family, there's a recipe here to suit. We've included some updated classics like *Caesar turkey burgers, Jerk pork & pineapple skewers* and *Coconut-crusted lime chicken*. Or why not dip into the tempting Flavours from Around the World chapter to try *Greek beans with seared lamb, Mexican rice with chipotle pork* or *Italian sausage & pasta pot*. Or you could choose a supper from the veggie section such as the scrumptious *Artichoke, red onion & rosemary risotto* or *Linguine with watercress & almond pesto*, and there are plenty of low-fat choices too.

Stir-frying is a fast and healthy way to cook lean cuts of meat, firm-textured fish and colourful crunchy vegetables; if you use a good-quality non-stick pan you only need to use a little oil. Make sure the pan and oil are really hot before you add the ingredients, then the food won't soak up the oil and will keep its flavour, colour and nutrients while it quickly cooks. If the mixture does start to stick, just add a tablespoon of water instead of any extra oil. Also, do all the chopping and slicing before you start to cook, ensuring the ingredients are cut to a similar size so they cook evenly.

All these recipes have been triple-tested by the *Good Food* team, so give them a go and tempt family and friends with your new wide range of super suppers.

*Sharon*

Sharon Brown
*Good Food* magazine

# Notes and conversion tables

## NOTES ON THE RECIPES
• Eggs are large in the UK and Australia and extra large in America unless stated otherwise.
• Wash fresh produce before preparation.
• Recipes contain nutritional analyses for 'sugar', which means the total sugar content including all natural sugars in the ingredients, unless otherwise stated.

## OVEN TEMPERATURES

| Gas | °C | °C Fan | °F | Oven temp. |
|-----|-----|--------|-----|------------|
| ¼ | 110 | 90 | 225 | Very cool |
| ½ | 120 | 100 | 250 | Very cool |
| 1 | 140 | 120 | 275 | Cool or slow |
| 2 | 150 | 130 | 300 | Cool or slow |
| 3 | 160 | 140 | 325 | Warm |
| 4 | 180 | 160 | 350 | Moderate |
| 5 | 190 | 170 | 375 | Moderately hot |
| 6 | 200 | 180 | 400 | Fairly hot |
| 7 | 220 | 200 | 425 | Hot |
| 8 | 230 | 210 | 450 | Very hot |
| 9 | 240 | 220 | 475 | Very hot |

## APPROXIMATE WEIGHT CONVERSIONS
• All the recipes in this book list both imperial and metric measurements. Conversions are approximate and have been rounded up or down. Follow one set of measurements only; do not mix the two.
• Cup measurements, which are used by cooks in Australia and America, have not been listed here as they vary from ingredient to ingredient. Kitchen scales should be used to measure dry/solid ingredients.

*Good Food* is concerned about sustainable sourcing and animal welfare. Where possible, humanely reared meats, sustainably caught fish (see fishonline. org for further information from the Marine Conservation Society) and free-range chickens and eggs are used when recipes are originally tested.

SPOON MEASURES

Spoon measurements are level unless otherwise specified.

• 1 teaspoon (tsp) = 5ml
• 1 tablespoon (tbsp) = 15ml
• 1 Australian tablespoon = 20ml (cooks in Australia should measure 3 teaspoons where 1 tablespoon is specified in a recipe)

APPROXIMATE LIQUID CONVERSIONS

| metric | imperial | AUS | US |
|--------|----------|-----|-----|
| 50ml | 2fl oz | ¼ cup | ¼ cup |
| 125ml | 4fl oz | ½ cup | ½ cup |
| 175ml | 6fl oz | ¾ cup | ¾ cup |
| 225ml | 8fl oz | 1 cup | 1 cup |
| 300ml | 10fl oz/½ pint | ½ pint | 1¼ cups |
| 450ml | 16fl oz | 2 cups | 2 cups/1 pint |
| 600ml | 20fl oz/1 pint | 1 pint | 2½ cups |
| 1 litre | 35fl oz/1¾ pints | 1¾ pints | 1 quart |

# Meatballs with spicy chipotle-tomato sauce

*Just a little chipotle paste adds a big smoky, spicy flavour to stews, soups and sauces.*
*This midweek family supper provides two of your 5-a-day.*

**TAKES 55 MINUTES ● SERVES 4**
500g/1lb 2oz minced pork
2 large handfuls fresh breadcrumbs
1 egg, beaten
2 medium red onions, ¼ finely
    chopped, the rest sliced
small bunch coriander leaves and
    stems, finely chopped separately,
    plus extra leaves to garnish
2 tbsp vegetable oil
2 garlic cloves, chopped
400ml/14fl oz passata
1 tbsp chipotle paste
potatoes or rice, to serve

**1** In a small bowl, mix together the pork, breadcrumbs, egg, finely chopped onion and the chopped coriander leaves. Season, mix well and shape into small meatballs.
**2** Add 1 tablespoon of the oil to a large frying pan and over a medium heat brown the meatballs on all sides, then remove from the pan and set aside.
**3** Add the remaining oil, the sliced onion, garlic, coriander stems and some salt. Cook for 5 minutes, then add the passata and chipotle paste. Pour in 100ml/3½fl oz water and stir well, then simmer for 10 minutes. Add the meatballs and cook for a further 5 minutes. Serve with potatoes or rice and scatter with the extra coriander leaves.

PER SERVING 406 kcals, protein 31g, carbs 26g, fat 20g, sat fat 6g, fibre 3g, sugar 10g, salt 1.5g

# Cod & tomato traybake

*This simple supper is cooked in just one baking tin so the washing up is minimal –*
*always a bonus! Plus it's healthy too as it provides four of your 5-a-day.*

**TAKES 45 MINUTES ● SERVES 4**

2 red peppers, deseeded and chopped
2 red onions, cut into wedges
250g/9oz cherry tomatoes
handful pitted black olives
½ × 680g jar passata
400g can butter beans, drained and
  rinsed
4 skinless cod fillets (about 600g/
  1lb 5oz in total)
small bunch basil
crusty bread, to serve (optional)

**1** Heat oven to 220C/200C fan/gas 7.
Put the peppers, onions, tomatoes and
olives into a large, deep baking tin and
cook for 15 minutes until they start to
soften and char at the edges.
**2** Stir in the passata, butter beans
and some seasoning, then make four
little hollows and nestle in the cod fillets.
Return to the oven and cook for a further
15 minutes until the cod is cooked
through. Sprinkle over the basil and
serve with crusty bread, if you like.

PER SERVING 284 kcals, protein 37g, carbs 27g,
fat 3g, sat fat 1g, fibre 8g, sugar 14g, salt 2.3g

# Buttery chilli prawns

*These prawns are good with some warm crusty bread. If you'd like to serve these as a starter, 12–16 prawns will be ample; as a main course 20 is more generous.*

**TAKES 25 MINUTES • SERVES 2**

25g/1oz butter

2 tbsp olive oil

3 garlic cloves, finely chopped

1 red chilli, seeds left in, finely chopped

½ tsp sweet paprika

12–20 large raw king prawns with
   shells

juice 1 lemon, plus a few slices for a
   finger bowl

½ small bunch parsley, roughly
   chopped

small loaf crusty bread, warmed, to
   serve

**1** Melt the butter and oil together in a frying pan. Add the garlic, chilli and paprika, then fry for 1–2 minutes until starting to turn golden. Turn up the heat, throw in the prawns and fry for a few minutes, stirring, until all the prawns turn pink. Take off the heat, season and stir in the lemon juice and parsley.

**2** Add some lemon slices to a finger bowl of warm water, grab a bowl for the shells, then dig straight in with your fingers and serve with hunks of crusty bread.

PER SERVING 237 kcals, protein 9g, carbs 2g, fat 22g, sat fat 8g, fibre 1g, sugar 1g, salt 1.6g

# Chicken & chorizo traybake

*The gutsy flavours of this all-in-one supper are perfect for a chilly evening. Easily doubled, this simple dish would be good for entertaining friends.*

**TAKES 55 MINUTES • SERVES 4**

140g/5oz cooking chorizo
2 red onions, cut into wedges
4 garlic cloves, left whole
4 chicken thighs, skin on
4 chicken drumsticks, skin on
4 medium potatoes, unpeeled and cut
   into wedges
2 rosemary sprigs
2 tbsp olive oil
crusty bread, to serve

**1** Heat oven to 220C/200C fan/gas 7. Cut the chorizo into slices the thickness of a pound coin. Put the onions and garlic in the bottom of a large roasting tin. Scatter over the chorizo, then add the chicken pieces, potatoes, rosemary and a couple of grinds of black pepper. Drizzle with the olive oil, then bake for 45 minutes.

**2** Halfway through the cooking time, give everything a good baste in the chorizo juices. Serve with hunks of crusty bread.

PER SERVING 489 kcals, protein 30g, carbs 23g, fat 30g, sat fat 9g, fibre 3g, sugar 6g, salt 0.8g

# Liver & bacon with onion gravy

*A really nutritious dish – one serving will provide your daily quota of iron, zinc, folate and vitamin C. Liver is a good source of B12, which helps your body to use iron.*

**TAKES 30 MINUTES ● SERVES 2**

4 rashers smoked streaky bacon
2 tbsp plain flour, seasoned
pinch dried sage (optional)
6 slices lamb's liver (about 400g/14oz
  in total)
1 tbsp olive oil
1 onion, thinly sliced
300ml/½ pint beef stock
2 tbsp ketchup
mashed potato, to serve

**1** Cook the bacon in a large non-stick frying pan until crisp. Meanwhile, mix the flour and sage, if using, and use to dust the liver. Remove the bacon from the pan and set aside. Add the oil to the pan and brown the liver for about 1 minute on each side. Remove from the pan, then fry the onion until softened. Stir in the stock and ketchup, then bubble for 5 minutes.

**2** Put the liver back in the pan and cook for 3 minutes until cooked through. Serve with the bacon broken over the top and some mash.

PER SERVING 504 kcals, protein 53g, carbs 23g, fat 23g, sat fat 7g, fibre 3g, sugar 7g, salt 2.5g

# Steamed mussels with cider & spring onions

*Serve these mussels with plenty of bread to mop up the creamy juices. Although available all year round, mussels are at their peak between October and March.*

**TAKES 30 MINUTES • SERVES 2**

900g/2lb live mussels
small knob butter
8 spring onions, chopped into 2cm/¾in
   pieces
2 garlic cloves, thinly sliced
250ml/9fl oz cider or perry
4 thyme sprigs
150ml/¼ pint single cream
25g/1oz flat-leaf parsley, chopped
crusty bread, to serve

**1** Wash the mussels in a colander to remove any dirt and grit. Pick through them, removing any stringy 'beards' from the shells. If any of the mussels are slightly open, tap them on the work surface to see if they close (which means they are still alive) and discard any that remain open.

**2** Melt the butter in a large heavy-based pan. Sauté the spring onions and garlic over a high heat for 1 minute before pouring in the cider or perry.

Add the thyme and the mussels, cover and cook for 3–4 minutes or until the mussels start to open. Add the cream, season and stir in the parsley.

**3** Divide the mussels between two bowls. Pour over the sauce and any spring onions left in the pan. Serve with crusty bread.

PER SERVING 586 kcals, protein 59g, carbs 19g, fat 27g, sat fat 14g, fibre 1g, sugar 8g, salt 3.4g

# Scrambled egg stir-fry

*If you want to make a veggie version of this, simply replace the prawns with chunks of tofu. You could also add some sliced mushrooms before the beansprouts.*

**TAKES 10 MINUTES • SERVES 2**

1 tbsp oil
100g/4oz cooked peeled prawns, defrosted if frozen
thumb-sized piece ginger, grated
large handful fresh beansprouts
4 spring onions, sliced
4 eggs, beaten
1 tbsp soy sauce, plus extra to taste

**1** Heat the oil in a wok or frying pan and stir-fry the prawns on a high heat for 30 seconds until they start to take on a little colour. Tip in the ginger, beansprouts and half of the spring onions, and stir-fry for another 30 seconds, then turn down the heat and pour in the eggs.

**2** Leave to set for a few seconds, then move the loosely set egg around the pan with a spatula to scramble. When all of the egg has set, tip in the soy sauce and let it sizzle for a few seconds. Serve sprinkled with the rest of the shredded spring onion and season with more soy sauce to taste.

PER SERVING 296 kcals, protein 28g, carbs 2g, fat 20g, sat fat 4g, fibre 1g, sugar 0.1g, salt 3.81g

# Thai prawn, ginger & spring onion stir-fry

*This stir-fry has a welcome spicy kick. Once you've made the paste, it takes only 10 minutes to cook and makes a perfect treat-for-two supper.*

**TAKES 40 MINUTES • SERVES 2**

200g/7oz raw peeled tiger prawns
1 green Thai chilli, chopped
3 garlic cloves, 1 crushed and 2 finely sliced
1 bunch coriander, leaves and stalks separated
1 tbsp caster sugar
juice 1 lime, plus extra wedges to garnish
3 tbsp Thai fish sauce
2 tbsp groundnut oil
3cm/1¼in piece ginger, finely sliced, then shredded
8 spring onions, finely sliced
1 red pepper, deseeded and thinly sliced
85g/3oz water chestnuts, sliced
100g/4oz beansprouts
1 tbsp soy sauce
egg or rice noodles, to serve

**1** Put the prawns in a bowl. Put the chilli, crushed garlic, coriander stalks (snipped up using scissors first) and sugar in a small food processor, and whizz together. Add half the lime juice and the fish sauce, then pour this over the prawns. Set aside.

**2** Heat 1 tablespoon of the oil in a wok, add the ginger, onions and sliced garlic, and fry for 1 minute. Add the red pepper and fry for 1 minute. Add the water chestnuts and beansprouts, and toss together until the beansprouts start to wilt. Add the soy sauce and some black pepper, then tip into a serving dish.

**3** Heat the remaining oil in the wok and add the prawns, lifting them out of their juices. Toss for 1–2 minutes until they turn pink. Add the marinade and swirl the wok quickly, then tip on to the veg. Snip over the coriander leaves and sprinkle with the remaining lime juice. Serve over noodles with lime wedges on the side.

PER SERVING 294 kcals, protein 25g, carbs 22g, fat 12g, sat fat 2g, fibre 3g, sugar 17g, salt 6.32g

# Hot-sour pork & pepper stir-fry

*A fresh, simple dish with loads of flavour and a lovely hint of lime. Much nicer than a gloopy sweet and sour from your local Chinese takeaway.*

**TAKES 25 MINUTES • SERVES 2**

1 tbsp sesame seeds
1 tsp sunflower oil
250g/9oz pork fillet, cut into finger-
    width strips
1 red and 1 yellow pepper, deseeded
    and sliced
2 tsp cornflour
2 tsp soy sauce
juice 1 lime
2 tbsp clear honey
½ red chilli, deseeded and sliced
steamed jasmine rice, to serve

**1** Dry-fry the sesame seeds until toasted and golden, then tip into a small bowl and set aside.

**2** Heat the oil in a non-stick frying pan or wok, add the pork and peppers, and stir-fry for 5–6 minutes over a high heat until the pork is lightly browned and cooked through. Mix the cornflour and soy sauce together in a bowl, then add the lime juice, honey, chilli and sesame seeds, plus 6 tablespoons cold water. Pour into the wok and cook until the sauce has slightly thickened, tossing the pan to coat the pork and peppers. Serve with jasmine rice.

PER SERVING 354 kcals, protein 31g, carbs 25g, fat 14.5g, sat fat 4g, fibre 4.3g, sugar 20.2g, salt 1.1g

# Summery chicken stir-fry

*Serve this easy stir-fry with some rice noodles cooked according to the pack instructions and then tossed in a little sesame oil. The cashews make a great crunchy addition.*

**TAKES 25 MINUTES** ● **SERVES 2**

handful cashew nuts
2 tbsp sunflower oil
2 boneless skinless chicken breasts,
    cut into thin strips
3 spring onions, sliced
175g/6oz small broccoli florets
175g/6oz sugar snap peas or
    mangetout
½ small head Chinese leaves, shredded
2 tbsp hoisin sauce

**1** Heat a wok or large frying pan. Add the cashews and fry until toasted. Remove and set aside.

**2** Add 1 tablespoon of the oil and the chicken to the wok, fry quickly until evenly browned, then remove from the pan. Add the remaining oil along with the spring onions and broccoli, and stir-fry quickly for 2–3 minutes, then add the peas or mangetout and Chinese leaves, and stir-fry for a further minute.

**3** Return the chicken to the pan with the hoisin sauce and 6 tablespoons water. Bring to the boil, then cover and cook for 5 minutes until the chicken is cooked through. Scatter over the nuts to serve.

PER SERVING 420 kcals, protein 45g, carbs 16g, fat 20g, sat fat 3g, fibre 6g, sugar 12g, salt 0.78g

# Mustard salmon & veg bake with horseradish

*The combination of parsnips, beetroots and carrots mean this dish includes three of your 5-a-day. Use your own favourite mix of root veg to ring the changes.*

**TAKES 40 MINUTES ● SERVES 4**

4 parsnips, sliced lengthways
4 small raw beetroots, thickly sliced
6 carrots, sliced lengthways
2 tbsp olive oil
4 × 125g/4½oz salmon fillets, skin on
2 tbsp grainy mustard
2 tbsp hot horseradish
150ml/¼ pint crème fraîche
1 tbsp cider vinegar
1 tbsp chopped dill

**1** Heat oven to 200C/180C fan/gas 6. Toss all the vegetables with the oil and season well. Spread in a single layer on two baking tins (or 1 very large one) and roast for 30 minutes.

**2** Season the salmon and spread the mustard over. In the final 10 minutes of cooking the veg, add the salmon to the tins.

**3** In a small bowl, mix together the horseradish, crème fraîche, vinegar, dill and some seasoning. Serve the salmon with the sauce and veg.

PER SERVING 587 kcals, protein 30g, carbs 31g, fat 38g, sat fat 14g, fibre 11g, sugar 22g, salt 0.8g

# Beef, mushroom & greens stir-fry

*Stir-frying is the quickest way to cook so it makes a perfect choice for midweek meals when time is short. This tasty supper is ready in just 20 minutes.*

**TAKES 20 MINUTES • SERVES 4**

4 tbsp oyster sauce
2 tbsp dark soy sauce
1–2 tbsp vegetable oil
400g/14oz beef rump steak, thinly
  sliced across the grain into
  0.5cm/¼in thick pieces
fingertip-length piece ginger, chopped
300g/10oz spring greens, sliced
150g pack chestnut mushrooms, sliced
boiled rice or noodles, to serve

**1** Mix the oyster and soy sauces together, and set aside. Heat a wok until smoking hot, add 1 teaspoon of the oil, then stir-fry the meat until browned all over. You may need to do this in two batches, adding a little more oil. Remove the meat, then wipe the wok clean.

**2** Add a little more oil. Stir-fry the ginger until golden, then add the spring greens and mushrooms. Cook for 3 minutes, stirring often, then add the steak and soy-sauce mixture. Cook for 3–4 more minutes until the sauce has thickened a little and everything is warmed through. Serve over rice or noodles.

PER SERVING 273 kcals, protein 25g, carbs 7g, fat 17g, sat fat 5g, fibre 3g, sugar 5g, salt 3.13g

# Sweet-chilli prawn stir-fry

*Spicy and crunchy, this stir-fry looks and tastes delicious, and has a savoury and sweet flavour. You can add more veg, if you like, such as sliced spring onions and mangetout.*

**TAKES 20 MINUTES • SERVES 2**

4 tbsp soft brown sugar
1 tbsp vegetable oil
1 head broccoli, cut into small florets
½ × 250g pack baby sweetcorn, halved
　　lengthways
2 tbsp Thai red curry paste
1 red pepper, deseeded and sliced
splash Thai fish sauce or low-salt soy
　　sauce
200g/7oz cooked peeled frozen
　　prawns, defrosted
boiled rice or noodles, to serve

**1** Tip the sugar into a wok, add a splash of water and let it dissolve over a low heat. Once dissolved, turn up the heat until it bubbles, then pour into a heatproof bowl.

**2** Heat the oil in the wok, then stir-fry the broccoli and sweetcorn together for 3 minutes until they start to brown slightly.

**3** Stir the curry paste into the caramel, then pour into the wok. Add the red pepper and continue to cook for 2 minutes. Splash in the fish sauce or soy, add the prawns and stir-fry again to heat through. Serve immediately with rice or noodles.

PER SERVING 386 kcals, protein 32g, carbs 41g, fat 12g, sat fat 1g, fibre 6g, sugar 39g, salt 2.22g

# Saucy beef stir-fry

*The quantities here can easily be doubled to serve six and you could also toss a bag of salad through before serving. The marinade works just as well with chicken or pork.*

**TAKES 30 MINUTES • SERVES 3**

500g/1lb 2oz stir-fry beef strips
2 tbsp balsamic vinegar
2 tbsp dark soy sauce
2 tbsp Worcestershire sauce
small bunch spring onions, sliced on
    the diagonal
200g/7oz roasted antipasto peppers in
    oil or vinegar, drained and sliced
boiled rice, to serve

**1** Put the beef in a medium non-metallic bowl and mix with the vinegar, soy and Worcestershire sauces. Leave to marinate for 20 minutes or, if you have the time, overnight.

**2** Heat a small, dry wok until it is very hot. Tip in the beef, marinade and spring onions, and stir-fry for 2 minutes. Add the roasted peppers, then stir-fry for a further 2 minutes. Divide the stir-fry among three shallow bowls and serve with some boiled rice.

PER SERVING 433 kcals, protein 38g, carbs 8g, fat 28g, sat fat 10g, fibre 1g, sugar 1g, salt 3.14g

# Fragrant courgette & prawn curry

*If you grow your own, this fabulously flavoured curry is a good way of using up courgettes. This spicy, summery one-pot is perfect for a busy weeknight.*

**TAKES 35 MINUTES • SERVES 2**

2 tbsp sunflower oil

500g/1lb 2oz courgettes, thickly sliced

½ tsp cumin seeds

2 tbsp finely chopped ginger

6 garlic cloves, crushed

1 red chilli, deseeded and finely
    chopped

1 tsp ground coriander

¼ tsp ground turmeric

500g/1lb 2oz tomatoes, chopped

150ml/¼ pint hot vegetable stock

225g pack raw peeled frozen jumbo
    prawns, defrosted

½ small bunch coriander, roughly
    chopped

basmati rice and mango chutney,
    to serve (optional)

**1** Heat the oil in a large wok and stir-fry the courgettes for 5–6 minutes until softened. Lift from the pan with a slotted spoon, leaving the oil behind. Set aside.

**2** Add the cumin seeds to the pan and toast for a few seconds, then add the ginger, garlic, chilli and spices. Cook, stirring, for 1–2 minutes, then tip in the chopped tomatoes and cook for a few minutes more.

**3** Pour in the stock and simmer to make a pulpy sauce, then add the courgettes and prawns. Cook gently until the prawns change from grey to pink and the courgettes are tender, but not too soft. Stir in most of the coriander, saving some to sprinkle over the top. Serve with some boiled basmati rice and a bowl of mango chutney, if you like.

PER SERVING 305 kcals, protein 28g, carbs 17g, fat 15g, sat fat 2g, fibre 5g, sugar 13g, salt 1.41g

# Stir-fried lamb with peppers

*This easy stir-fry makes a healthy supper for two and packs in three of your 5-a-day. For a change, try lean sliced beef instead of the lamb.*

**TAKES 35 MINUTES** • **SERVES 2**

200g/7oz lean lamb fillet, trimmed of any visible fat and cut into thin strips
2.5cm/1in piece ginger, grated
1 garlic clove, crushed
4 spring onions, chopped
2 tbsp black bean sauce
2 tsp olive oil
1 red onion, peeled and cut into thin wedges
1 red pepper, deseeded and thinly sliced
1 green pepper, deseeded and thinly sliced
6 small broccoli florets
2 tsp sesame seeds
boiled rice or noodles, to serve

**1** In a deep bowl, mix the lamb strips with the ginger, garlic, spring onions and black bean sauce. Leave to marinate in the fridge for 15 minutes.

**2** Heat the olive oil in a wok or large non-stick frying pan over a medium heat. Add the lamb, marinade ingredients and the onion wedges, and stir-fry for 5 minutes, until the meat starts to brown. Add the peppers and broccoli, and stir-fry for 5 minutes, stirring often until the lamb is tender and the veg cooked. Serve sprinkled with sesame seeds, with noodles or rice.

PER SERVING 302 kcals, protein 27g, carbs 14g, fat 16g, sat fat 5g, fibre 5g, sugar 12g, salt 1.17g

# Stir-fry prawns with peppers & spinach

*This is a brilliant speedy supper for two. Pick up the ingredients on your way home from work, throw them into the wok and serve with instant egg noodles.*

**TAKES 15 MINUTES • SERVES 2**

3 tbsp groundnut or sunflower oil
2 fat garlic cloves, thinly sliced
1 small red pepper, deseeded and
  thinly sliced
200g pack raw peeled tiger frozen
  prawns, patted dry
2 tbsp soy or Thai fish sauce
100g bag baby leaf spinach

**1** Heat a wok until you can feel a good heat rising. Add 2 tablespoons of the oil and, a few seconds later, the garlic slices. Stir-fry until they start to turn golden, then using a slotted spoon, spoon on to kitchen paper to drain.

**2** Toss in the red pepper and stir-fry for 1 minute or so until softened, then scoop out and set aside. Add the remaining tablespoon of oil. Heat, then toss in the prawns and stir-fry for another 2–3 minutes until cooked and just beginning to brown. Add the soy or fish sauce.

**3** Throw in the spinach and stir-fry until it begins to wilt. Return the peppers and garlic to the wok. Serve immediately.

PER SERVING 269 kcals, protein 21g, carbs 7g, fat 18g, sat fat 3g, fibre 2g, sugar none, salt 3.38g

# Chicken with mushrooms

*The pancetta adds a wonderful flavour to this supper, and the chicken thighs stay superbly moist. Creamy mash would be a perfect accompaniment.*

**TAKES 40 MINUTES • SERVES 4**

2 tbsp olive oil
500g/1lb 2oz boneless skinless chicken
  thighs
flour, for dusting
50g/2oz cubetti di pancetta
300g/10oz small button mushrooms
2 large shallots, chopped
250ml/9fl oz chicken stock
1 tbsp white wine vinegar
50g/2oz frozen peas
small handful parsley, finely chopped

**1** Heat 1 tablespoon of the oil in a frying pan. Season and dust the chicken with flour. Brown the chicken on all sides in the pan. Remove. Fry the pancetta and mushrooms until softened, then remove.
**2** Add the remaining oil and cook the shallots for 5 minutes. Add the stock and vinegar, and bubble for 1–2 minutes. Return the chicken, pancetta and mushrooms to the pan and cook for 15 minutes. Add the peas and parsley to the wok, and cook for 2 minutes more, then serve.

PER SERVING 260 kcals, protein 32g, carbs 3g, fat 13g, sat fat 3g, fibre 3g, sugar 1g, salt 0.9g

# Smoky pork & black bean tacos

*Put the spicy pork, lettuce, avocado and soured cream on the table, and let everyone help themselves and fill up their own warm tacos.*

**TAKES 25 MINUTES • SERVES 4**

2 tsp vegetable oil
½ red onion, chopped
2 tsp smoked paprika
2 tsp ground cumin
500g pack lean minced pork
300ml/½ pint passata
5 tbsp barbecue sauce
400g can black beans, drained and
    rinsed
small bunch coriander, chopped
8 taco shells
1 ripe avocado, peeled and sliced
½ iceberg lettuce, finely shredded
soured cream, to garnish

**1** Heat the oil in a large frying pan, add the onion and cook for 5 minutes until softened. Sprinkle over the spices and cook for 1 minute more. Add the mince, breaking it up with the back of a wooden spoon, and stir until cooked through.

**2** Stir the passata and barbecue sauce into the pan along with 4 tablespoons water. Increase the heat and allow the sauce to bubble and reduce until it clings to the meat. Add the beans, season and cook for a further 2 minutes, then stir in the coriander. Heat the tacos according to the pack instructions.

**3** Use the pork and bean mix to fill the tacos, top with slices of avocado, shredded iceberg lettuce and a dollop of soured cream.

PER SERVING 592 kcals, protein 38g, carbs 45g, fat 29g, sat fat 7g, fibre 10g, sugar 12g, salt 1.4g

# Potato frittata with pesto & goat's cheese

*This easy recipe makes a great midweek supper with a good mix of flavours and textures. Make sure the pesto you use is suitable for vegetarians.*

**TAKES 35 MINUTES • SERVES 4**

4 medium potatoes (about 600g/
    1lb 5oz in total), thinly sliced
1 garlic clove, finely chopped
8 eggs, lightly beaten
1 tbsp olive oil
100g pack soft rindless goat's cheese,
    sliced
3 tbsp pesto, to drizzle
handful rocket leaves, to garnish
tomato and basil salad, to serve
    (optional)

**1** Boil the potatoes in a pan of boiling salted water for 5 minutes until just tender. Meanwhile, heat oven to 220C/200C fan/gas 7. Mix the garlic and eggs together with some seasoning, then drain the potatoes and stir into the egg.

**2** Heat the oil in an ovenproof frying pan, then tip in the egg-and-potato mixture. Cook over a low heat for 5 minutes or until two-thirds of the frittata is set, then place in the oven for 10–15 minutes until cooked through.

**3** Arrange the goat's cheese round the edge of the frittata and drizzle with the pesto. Top with rocket and serve with a tomato and basil salad, if you like.

PER SERVING 426 kcals, protein 23g, carbs 25g, fat 26g, sat fat 8g, fibre 2g, sugar 1g, salt 0.9g

# Courgette & ricotta pasta

*Here's a real summery take on a pasta supper. Courgettes, lemon, basil and ricotta make a light dish suitable for a sun-filled day.*

**TAKES 30 MINUTES • SERVES 4**

2 tbsp olive oil
1 shallot, finely chopped
4 courgettes, halved and thinly sliced
3 garlic cloves, finely chopped
300g/10oz pasta shapes
small bunch basil, most chopped
zest 1 lemon
50g/2oz vegetarian Parmesan-style
   cheese, grated, plus extra to garnish
   (optional)
50g/2oz pine nuts, toasted
250g tub ricotta

**1** Heat the oil in a large frying pan. Cook the shallot and courgettes for 8 minutes until softened. When they are just beginning to colour, add the garlic and cook for 2 minutes more.

**2** Cook the pasta according to the pack instructions. Drain, reserving a little of the water. Tip the pasta into the courgette pan with the basil, lemon zest, grated cheese and pine nuts. Season, dot over the ricotta and mix gently so that you don't break it up too much. Serve sprinkled with extra grated cheese, if you like.

PER SERVING 511 kcals, protein 23g, carbs 43g, fat 27g, sat fat 8g, fibre 2g, sugar 5g, salt 0.5g

# Pasta with chilli tomatoes & spinach

*Wholemeal pasta has a nice nutty flavour, but it does take longer to cook so check the pack instructions. Add enough chilli flakes to suit your own love of spiciness.*

**TAKES 30 MINUTES • SERVES 2**

2 tsp olive oil

1 onion, finely chopped

2 garlic cloves, crushed

½ tsp dried chilli flakes

200g/7oz wholemeal penne pasta

400g can chopped tomatoes

100ml/3½fl oz red wine

½ tsp dried oregano

125g bag baby leaf spinach

25g/1oz vegetarian Parmesan-style cheese, grated

**1** Heat the oil in a non-stick frying pan and gently fry the onion, garlic and chilli flakes, stirring regularly, for 5 minutes (add a little water if they begin to stick).

**2** Cook the pasta according to the pack instructions. Add the tomatoes, wine and oregano to the frying pan, and stir to combine. Bring to a gentle simmer and cook, stirring occasionally, for 10 minutes.

**3** Shake the spinach into the pan and cook for 1–2 minutes until wilted. Drain the pasta and tip into the pan with the sauce. Toss to combine, sprinkle with cheese and serve.

PER SERVING 524 kcals, protein 24g, carbs 75g, fat 11g, sat fat 3g, fibre 13g, sugar 13g, salt 0.7g

# Cheesy bean & sweetcorn cakes with quick salsa

*Children love these crispy cakes. If you have any left over, tuck them into a school lunchbox the next day. Double the recipe, and you can freeze half for another meal.*

**TAKES 30 MINUTES • SERVES 4**

400g can mixed beans in water, drained and rinsed

400g can chickpeas, drained and rinsed

50g/2oz mature Cheddar, grated

198g can sweetcorn, drained

8 jalapeño slices from a jar, finely chopped

1 egg, beaten

small handful coriander, chopped

2 tbsp vegetable oil

10 cherry tomatoes, quartered

½ red onion, sliced

juice ½ lime

mixed salad leaves, to serve (optional)

**1** Put the beans and chickpeas in the bowl of a food processor and blend until smooth. Tip into a bowl and add the cheese, sweetcorn, jalapeños, egg and half the coriander. Season, mix well to combine, then shape into eight patties.

**2** Heat the oil in a large frying pan and cook the patties for 4 minutes on each side – you may have to do this in batches. Keep them warm in the oven as you go.

**3** Mix the tomatoes, onion, remaining coriander and the lime juice with a little salt. Serve the cakes with the salsa and some mixed salad leaves, if you like.

PER SERVING 292 kcals, protein 17g, carbs 24g, fat 13g, sat fat 4g, fibre 12g, sugar 2g, salt 1.9g

# Linguine with watercress & almond pesto

*The velvety pesto coats the linguine perfectly, and the little nuggets of almonds and cheese just add to the pleasure of this delicious new idea for a pasta supper for two.*

**TAKES 17 MINUTES • SERVES 2**

200g/7oz linguine or spaghetti
85g bag watercress
1 garlic clove, roughly chopped
25g/1oz vegetarian Parmesan-style
   cheese, ½ grated, ½ shaved
50g/2oz toasted flaked almonds
4 tbsp extra virgin olive oil
1 tbsp lemon juice
½ tsp sugar

**1** Cook the pasta according to the pack instructions. Meanwhile, put the watercress and garlic in the bowl of a food processor and blend for a few seconds until finely chopped. Add the grated cheese, half the almonds, the olive oil, lemon juice and sugar. Season well, then blend until you have a smooth purée consistency.

**2** When the linguine or spaghetti is cooked, drain, reserving a cup of the cooking water. Return the pasta to the pan and pour over the pesto, using a little pasta water to loosen the sauce if necessary. Stir everything together and divide between two bowls. To serve, top with the shaved cheese and the remaining almonds.

PER SERVING 766 kcals, protein 23g, carbs 79g, fat 40g, sat fat 7g, fibre 7g, sugar 5g, salt 0.3g

# Roasted squash with pesto & mozzarella

*A modern mix of fresh flavours – spicy roasted squash combines beautifully with cool, creamy mozzarella and pesto to make this a perfect lunch for friends.*

**TAKES 55 MINUTES • SERVES 4**

1 small butternut squash, peeled, halved and sliced into 2cm/¾in thick slices

3 tsp olive oil

1 tsp dried crushed chillies

1 red onion, cut into thin wedges

2 red peppers, deseeded and cut into chunky pieces

50g bag rocket leaves

juice ½ lemon

125g ball light mozzarella

4 tbsp fresh pesto

**1** Heat oven to 220C/200C fan/gas 7. Put the squash on a large baking sheet. Toss with 2 teaspoons of the oil, the chillies and some seasoning. Bake for 15 minutes.

**2** Take the tin out of the oven and turn the squash. Scatter the onion and peppers over the top, and return to the oven for a further 25 minutes or until the vegetables are tender and lightly charred.

**3** Toss the rocket leaves with the remaining oil, the lemon juice and some pepper. Pile on to four plates and divide the squash, onion and peppers on top. Tear the mozzarella over the vegetables and spoon over the pesto. Serve warm.

PER SERVING 277 kcals, protein 13g, carbs 26g, fat 14g, sat fat 3g, fibre 5g, sugar 16g, salt 0.4g

# Spinach & chickpea curry

*This quick-to-make curry is packed with goodness – a good source of fibre, iron and folate, plus it delivers two of your 5-a-day. Use a hotter curry paste, if you prefer.*

**TAKES 20 MINUTES** ● **SERVES 4**

2 tbsp mild curry paste
1 onion, chopped
400g can cherry tomatoes
2 × 400g cans chickpeas, drained and
   rinsed
250g bag baby leaf spinach
squeeze lemon juice
boiled basmati rice, to serve

**1** Heat the curry paste in a large non-stick frying pan. Once it starts to split, add the onion and cook for 2 minutes to soften. Tip in the tomatoes and bubble for 5 minutes or until the sauce has reduced.

**2** Add the chickpeas and some seasoning, then cook for 1 minute more. Take off the heat, then tip in the spinach and allow the heat of the pan to wilt the leaves. Season, add the lemon juice and serve with basmati rice.

PER SERVING 203 kcals, protein 9g, carbs 28g, fat 4g, sat fat none, fibre 6g, sugar 5g, salt 1.5g

# Halloumi-aubergine burgers with harissa relish

*A perfect supper for a busy weeknight. Halloumi cheese makes a good standby to keep in the fridge, and it works perfectly here with the spicy caramelized-onion relish.*

**TAKES 20 MINUTES ● SERVES 4**

2½ tbsp olive oil

2 onions, very finely sliced

½ aubergine, cut into 8 round slices

250g block halloumi, cut into 8 slices

1 tbsp soft brown sugar

1 roasted red pepper from a jar, chopped

2 tsp harissa paste

4 ciabatta rolls, halved and lightly toasted

4 tbsp houmous

**1** Add 1 tablespoon of the oil to a pan and tip in the onions. Cook over a high heat for a few minutes, then turn down the heat and cook until soft and golden – about 8 minutes.

**2** Meanwhile, heat another tablespoon of the oil in a frying pan and fry the aubergine slices for a few minutes on each side until tender. Set aside. In the remaining oil, fry the halloumi until golden brown.

**3** Tip the brown sugar, red pepper and harissa into the onions. Cook for 1 minute until the sugar has melted. While the relish is cooking, spread the rolls with houmous, laying halloumi and aubergine slices on top. Spoon over the sticky, spicy relish and serve.

PER SERVING 510 kcals, protein 22g, carbs 39g, fat 29g, sat fat 12g, fibre 5g, sugar 12g, salt 3.2g

# Spiced cauliflower with chickpeas, herbs & pine nuts

*The pine nuts add crunch to this main-meal salad, while the maple syrup gives a hint of sweetness in the mustardy dressing. Good cold in a lunchbox too.*

**TAKES 50 MINUTES • SERVES 4**

1 large head cauliflower, broken into
   florets (about 1kg/2lb 4oz in total)
2 garlic cloves, crushed
2 tsp caraway seeds
2 tsp cumin seeds
3 tbsp olive oil
400g can chickpeas, drained and rinsed
100g/4oz pine nuts
small bunch each parsley and dill,
   leaves torn

**FOR THE DRESSING**

2 tbsp maple syrup
6 tbsp olive oil
1 heaped tsp wholegrain mustard

**1** Heat oven to 200C/180C fan/gas 6. Toss the cauliflower, garlic, spices, 2 tablespoons of the oil and some seasoning in a roasting tin, then roast for 30 minutes.

**2** Add the chickpeas, pine nuts and remaining oil to the cauliflower, then cook for 10 minutes more. Whisk together the dressing ingredients with some seasoning.

**3** Stir the herbs and dressing into the cauliflower and serve.

PER SERVING 590 kcals, protein 17g, carbs 27g, fat 46g, sat fat 5g, fibre 10g, sugar 14g, salt 0.6g

# Squash, lentil & bean one-pot with fig raita

*This dish is a real winner for veggies – a good source of iron, fibre, calcium and vitamin C, plus it meets your 5-a-day target. What's more, it tastes truly wonderful!*

**TAKES 45 MINUTES • SERVES 2**

400g/14oz piece butternut squash, peeled, deseeded and chunkily diced
1 onion, sliced
1 tbsp olive oil
2 tsp ground cumin
½ tsp chilli flakes
400g can chopped tomatoes
100g/4oz red split lentils
2 tsp agave syrup or brown sugar
2 tsp red or white wine vinegar
400g can kidney beans, drained and rinsed
2 dried figs, finely chopped
150g pot fat-free natural yogurt
½ small bunch parsley, chopped

**1** Fry the squash and onion in the oil for 5–8 minutes until the onion is softened. Stir in the cumin and chilli for 1 minute.

**2** Add the tomatoes plus a canful of water from the tomato can, the lentils, agave or sugar and vinegar. Bring to a simmer and cook for 10 minutes, then stir in the beans and cook for a further few minutes until the lentils are tender and the beans heated through.

**3** Meanwhile, mix together the figs, yogurt and parsley. Season the stew, then serve in bowls with the fig raita on the side.

---

PER SERVING 540 kcals, protein 28g, carbs 83g, fat 9g, sat fat 2g, fibre 15g, sugar 40g, salt 1.2g

# Courgette & quinoa-stuffed peppers

*Just six ingredients are all you need for this speedy summer meal. Quinoa is good for vegetarians as it is high in protein and makes a tasty alternative to rice.*

**TAKES 30 MINUTES • SERVES 4**

4 red peppers
1½ tbsp olive oil
1 courgette, quartered lengthways and
  thinly sliced
2 × 250g packs ready-to-eat quinoa
85g/3oz feta, finely crumbled
handful parsley, roughly chopped
green salad, to serve

**1** Heat oven to 200C/180C fan/gas 6. Cut each pepper in half through the stem and remove the seeds. Put the peppers, cut-side up, on a baking sheet, drizzle with 1 tablespoon of the olive oil and season well. Roast for 15 minutes.

**2** Meanwhile, heat the remaining oil in a small frying pan, add the courgette and cook until soft. Remove from the heat, then stir through the quinoa, feta and parsley. Season with pepper.

**3** Divide the quinoa mixture among the pepper halves, then return to the oven for 5 minutes to heat through. Serve with a green salad.

PER SERVING 260 kcals, protein 11g, carbs 33g, fat 8g, sat fat 3g, fibre 11g, sugar 10g, salt 0.8g

# Tofu, greens & cashew stir-fry

*Packed with veg, this supper includes all of your 5-a-day. Ready-marinated tofu is perfect for stir-fries as it is usually flavoured with soy sauce, garlic and ginger.*

**TAKES 20 MINUTES • SERVES 4**

1 tbsp vegetable oil
1 head broccoli, cut into small florets
4 garlic cloves, sliced
1 red chilli, deseeded and finely sliced
1 bunch spring onions, sliced
140g/5oz soya beans
2 heads pak choi, quartered
2 × 150g packs marinated tofu pieces
1½ tbsp hoisin sauce
1 tbsp reduced-salt soy sauce (add extra to suit your own taste)
25g/1oz roasted cashew nuts

**1** Heat the oil in a non-stick wok. Add the broccoli, then fry on a high heat for 5 minutes or until just tender, adding a little water if it begins to catch.

**2** Add the garlic and chilli, fry for 1 minute, then toss through the spring onions, soya beans, pak choi and tofu. Stir-fry for 2–3 minutes. Add the hoisin, soy and nuts to warm through, then serve at once.

PER SERVING 358 kcals, protein 25g, carbs 13g, fat 23g, sat fat 3g, fibre 6g, sugar 8g, salt 3.49g

# Spinach & courgette frittata

*Serve warm for lunch with a salad and crusty bread, or pack up to take to a picnic. Hot or cold, this frittata is just as good and delivers two of your 5-a-day.*

**TAKES 35 MINUTES ● SERVES 4**

1 tbsp olive oil
1 onion, sliced
1 tsp dried chilli flakes
350g/12oz courgettes, sliced
200g bag spinach leaves
125g/4½oz ricotta
6 medium eggs
salad leaves, to serve

**1** Heat the oil in a large ovenproof frying pan and cook the onion until soft. Add the chilli flakes and courgettes, and cook for 5 minutes more.

**2** Tip the spinach into a large colander and pour over a kettle of boiling water. Cool under cold running water, then squeeze dry. Scatter the spinach into the frying pan, then dot over the ricotta.

**3** Heat the grill to high. Beat the eggs with seasoning, pour into the pan and cook until almost completely set. Finish under the grill for 3 minutes or until golden and cooked through. Serve with some salad leaves.

PER SERVING 211 kcals, protein 15g, carbs 6g, fat 15g, sat fat 5g, fibre 3g, sugar 5g, salt 0.5g

# Brown-rice stir-fry with coriander omelette

*This dish is guaranteed to perk up a packet of brown rice. Remember to check the packet instructions, as brown rice takes longer to cook than white.*

**TAKES 45 MINUTES** • **SERVES 4**

200g/7oz brown basmati rice
1 tbsp rapeseed oil
thumb-size piece ginger, grated
3 garlic cloves, finely chopped
1 bunch spring onions, finely sliced
lengthways
150g pack shiitake mushrooms, sliced
2 carrots, finely sliced into sticks
1 red pepper, deseeded and finely
sliced
3 eggs, beaten with a splash of
skimmed milk
small handful chopped coriander, plus
extra leaves to garnish
2 tsp soy sauce
1 tsp toasted sesame oil
2 tbsp chilli jam
1 tbsp sesame seeds, toasted

**1** Cook the rice according to the pack instructions. Heat 2 teaspoons of the oil in a large frying pan or wok. Add the ginger and garlic, and fry for 1 minute. Tip in the veg and stir-fry over a high heat for 3–4 minutes.

**2** Meanwhile, mix the eggs with the coriander and seasoning. Heat a small non-stick frying pan with the remaining oil. Add the egg, stir once, then allow to cook over a gentle heat until almost set. Flip (using a plate if necessary) and cook on the other side until cooked through. Tip out on to a board and cut into strips.

**3** Add the drained cooked rice, soy sauce, sesame oil and chilli jam to the veg, mixing to heat through. Divide into four bowls and top with the omelette strips, a few coriander leaves and sesame seeds.

PER SERVING 351 kcals, protein 13g, carbs 50g, fat 13g, sat fat 2g, fibre 4g, sugar 13g, salt 0.73g

# Artichoke, red onion & rosemary risotto

*The rosemary lends a wonderful aroma to the risotto, and the artichoke hearts add an interesting texture to the creaminess. This is a healthy, low-fat version of a classic.*

**TAKES 50 MINUTES ● SERVES 4**

1 tbsp olive oil

2 red onions, sliced into thin wedges

2 red peppers, deseeded and cut into chunks

2 tbsp rosemary needles

140g/5oz arborio risotto rice

150ml/¼ pint white wine

850ml/1½ pints low-salt vegetable stock

400g can artichoke hearts in water, drained and halved

2 tbsp grated vegetarian Parmesan-style cheese

2 tbsp toasted pine nuts

**1** Heat the oil in a large frying pan or wok. Cook the onions gently for 6–7 minutes until softened and browning. Add the peppers and rosemary, and cook for a further 5 minutes. Add the rice and stir well.

**2** Pour in the wine and a third of the stock. Bring to the boil then reduce the heat and simmer gently, stirring occasionally until almost all the liquid is absorbed.

**3** Stir in another third of the stock and simmer again, until it is all absorbed. Add the final third with the artichokes and simmer again until the rice is tender.

**4** Season and stir in the cheese and half the pine nuts. Scatter over the remainder and serve.

PER SERVING 299 kcals, protein 9g, carbs 44g, fat 10g, sat fat 2g, fibre 4g, sugar 9g, salt 0.65g

# Chestnut & herb pesto pasta with mushrooms

*This seasonal pesto is a good way of using up any leftover herbs. Replacing olive with rapeseed oil helps bring through the chestnut flavour.*

**TAKES 25 MINUTES • SERVES 6**

100g/4oz cooked peeled chestnuts
handful each basil, parsley and mint,
    leaves only
50g/2oz vegetarian Parmesan-style
    cheese, grated, plus extra to garnish
    (optional)
2 garlic cloves
150ml/¼ pint rapeseed oil
500g/1lb 2oz dried pasta
1 tbsp olive oil
250g pack chestnut mushrooms,
    quartered

**1** Put the chestnuts in a food processor and pulse until roughly chopped. Throw in the herbs, cheese and garlic, then pulse again until chopped (not too finely). Pour in the rapeseed oil, mix together and season to taste.

**2** Cook the pasta in plenty of boiling salted water, according to the pack instructions. Meanwhile, heat the olive oil in a large frying pan and fry the mushrooms with some seasoning for 6–8 minutes until tender and starting to brown. When the pasta is cooked, drain it, return to the pan, then stir through the chestnut pesto and the mushrooms. Serve with some extra cheese on top, if you like.

PER SERVING 582 kcals, protein 14g, carbs 70g, fat 29g, sat fat 4g, fibre 4g, sugar 3g, salt 0.20g

# Moroccan-roasted veg with tahini dressing

*The delicious tahini-and-lemon dressing adds a zing to the spicy roasted vegetables. Easily doubled to serve a get-together with friends.*

**TAKES 45 MINUTES • SERVES 4**

2 courgettes, cut into chunks

3 red peppers, deseeded and cut into chunks

1 large aubergine, cut into chunks

8 spring onions, cut into 2cm/¾in lengths

2 tbsp olive oil

2 tbsp harissa paste

2 tbsp tahini

juice 1 lemon

4 tbsp Greek yogurt

small bunch mint, roughly chopped

couscous and pitta bread, to serve

**1** Heat oven to 200C/180C fan/gas 6. Spread the vegetables out on a baking sheet. Drizzle over the oil and harissa, season and toss well. Roast for 30 minutes or until cooked and beginning to caramelise.

**2** Mix together the tahini, lemon juice, yogurt and 1–2 tablespoons water to make a dressing. Stir in half the mint.

**3** Sprinkle the veg with the remaining mint and serve with the dressing, some couscous and warm pitta bread.

PER SERVING 272 kcals, protein 10g, carbs 15g, fat 19g, sat fat 5g, fibre 10g, sugar 14g, salt 0.2g

# Lemon chicken with fruity olive couscous

*This is a perfect dish to double up and then use the leftovers for packed lunches the following day. The olives and sultanas liven up the easy-make couscous.*

**TAKES 30 MINUTES • SERVES 4**

4 boneless skinless chicken breasts
juice 2 lemons
2 tbsp olive oil
1 tsp dried chilli flakes
3 garlic cloves, crushed

**FOR THE COUSCOUS**

200g/7oz couscous
85g/3oz sultanas
250ml/9fl oz hot chicken stock
85g/3oz pitted green olives
400g can chickpeas, drained and rinsed
2 tbsp chopped flat-leaf parsley

**1** Butterfly the chicken breasts by cutting through the thickest part of the breast, stopping 1cm/½in before the edge, then opening them out like a book. Whisk together the lemon juice, olive oil, chilli flakes and garlic. Pour half over the chicken and marinate for 15 minutes.

**2** Meanwhile, put the couscous and sultanas in a bowl, then pour over the stock. Cover the bowl with cling film and leave for 5 minutes.

**3** Heat a griddle or non-stick frying pan, remove the chicken from the marinade and cook for 4 minutes on each side until golden and cooked through.

**4** Fluff up the couscous with a fork and stir in the olives, chickpeas, parsley and remaining marinade. Season and serve with the chicken.

PER SERVING 460 kcals, protein 39g, carbs 49g, fat 11g, sat fat 2g, fibre 4g, sugar 15g, salt 2.1g

# Stir-fried pork with ginger & honey

*This easy stir-fry makes a great treat for two. You can ring the changes and replace the pork with chicken or beef. For added heat, stir in a sliced green chilli.*

**TAKES 25 MINUTES ● SERVES 2**

2 nests medium egg noodles
2 tsp cornflour
2 tbsp soy sauce
1 tbsp clear honey
1 tbsp sunflower oil
250g/9oz pork tenderloin, cut into bite-sized pieces
thumb-sized piece ginger, finely chopped
2 garlic cloves, finely chopped
1 green pepper, deseeded and sliced
100g/4oz mangetout
1 tsp sesame seeds, to garnish

**1** Bring a pan of salted water to the boil and cook the noodles according to the pack instructions.

**2** Meanwhile, mix the cornflour with 1 tablespoon water in a small bowl, then stir in the soy sauce and honey, and set aside.

**3** Heat the oil in a wok over a high heat. Add the pork and cook for 2 minutes until browned all over. Add the ginger, garlic, pepper and mangetout, and cook for a further 2 minutes. Reduce the heat, then add the soy-and-honey mixture, stirring and cooking until the sauce bubbles and thickens.

**4** Divide the drained noodles between two bowls. Top with the pork and vegetables, and finish with a sprinkling of sesame seeds.

PER SERVING 466 kcals, protein 36g, carbs 54g, fat 11g, sat fat 2g, fibre 4g, sugar 14g, salt 2.6g

# Herby pork with apple & chicory salad

*Fancy something a bit special for a Saturday night dinner with friends? This pork dish is easy and quick to cook, and works really well with the crisp and crunchy salad.*

**TAKES 35 MINUTES ● SERVES 4**

400g/14oz pork tenderloin, trimmed of
   any fat and sinew
1 tbsp walnut oil
2 tsp wholegrain mustard
1 tbsp each chopped tarragon and
   parsley
juice 1 lemon
1 tbsp clear honey
2 large eating apples, cored and sliced
270g pack chicory, leaves separated

**1** Heat oven to 200C/180C fan/gas 6. Rub the pork with 1 teaspoon of the oil, 1 teaspoon of the mustard and some seasoning. Add to a hot frying pan and quickly brown all over. Transfer the pork to a roasting tin and press on half the herbs. Roast for 15 minutes until just cooked.

**2** To make the salad, mix the lemon juice, honey and remaining walnut oil and mustard together. Season and toss through the apples, chicory and remaining herbs. Serve the pork sliced, with the salad on the side.

PER SERVING 215 kcals, protein 23g, carbs 15g, fat 8g, sat fat 2g, fibre 2g, sugar 14g, salt 0.3g

# Singapore noodles

*Using ready-prepared packs of stir-fry veg saves time when you're in a hurry, and you get a good selection. You could use chicken instead of pork for a change.*

**TAKES 45 MINUTES** ● **SERVES 4**

3 tbsp teriyaki sauce
½ tsp Chinese five-spice powder
2 tsp medium Madras curry powder
300g/10oz pork tenderloin, trimmed of any fat
140g/5oz medium egg noodles
1 tbsp sunflower oil
2 × 300g packs fresh mixed stir-fry vegetables
100g/4oz cooked peeled prawns, thawed if frozen

**1** Mix the teriyaki sauce, five-spice and curry powders. Add half to the pork, turning to coat, and leave to marinate for 15 minutes.

**2** Heat oven to 200C/180C fan/gas 6. Remove the pork from the marinade and put in a small roasting tin lined with foil. Roast for 15–20 minutes.

**3** Meanwhile, cook the noodles according to the pack instructions, but reduce the cooking time by 1 minute. Refresh in cold water and drain thoroughly.

**4** Transfer the pork to a chopping board and rest for 5 minutes. Set a large non-stick frying pan or wok over a medium–high heat. Add the oil and stir-fry the veg for 3–4 minutes. Cut the pork in half lengthways, then thinly slice. Tip into the pan, with the prawns, noodles and remaining marinade. Toss together for 2–3 minutes until hot.

PER SERVING 293 kcals, protein 27g, carbs 32g, fat 6g, sat fat 1g, fibre 4g, sugar 7g, salt 1.7g

# Harissa turkey kofta & carrot pittas

*Turkey mince makes a good low-fat choice. Harissa adds a spicy and fragrant flavour to the koftas but add it to suit your own taste – a little goes a long way.*

**TAKES 25 MINUTES ● MAKES 4**

500g pack minced turkey breast
1 heaped tbsp harissa paste
handful coriander, finely chopped
1 red onion, ½ grated, ½ thinly sliced
1 tbsp olive oil
2 tsp cumin seeds
3 carrots, cut into thin matchsticks
4 tbsp Greek-style yogurt
1 garlic clove, crushed
4 wholemeal pitta breads, lightly
   toasted and cut in half

**1** Heat the grill. In a large bowl, mix the mince, harissa, coriander, grated onion and some seasoning. Shape into eight small koftas. Lay on a baking sheet and grill for 6–8 minutes until cooked through, turning occasionally.

**2** Meanwhile, heat the oil in a pan, add the cumin seeds and toast for a minute or so until aromatic. Tip in the carrots, season and sauté for 5 minutes until just tender.

**3** Mix the yogurt and garlic. Stuff the pitta halves with the koftas, carrots, onion slices and garlicky yogurt to serve.

---

PER PITTA 464 kcals, protein 48g, carbs 42g, fat 12g, sat fat 5g, fibre 9g, sugar 15g, salt 0.9g

# Pineapple, beef & ginger stir-fry

*The spicy–sweet combo is scrummy here. If you want to add more veg, try half a thinly sliced red pepper or some shredded mangetout.*

**TAKES 25 MINUTES • SERVES 2**

400g/14oz rump steak, thinly sliced

3 tbsp soy sauce

2 tbsp soft brown sugar

1 tbsp chilli sauce

1 tbsp rice wine vinegar

2 tsp vegetable oil

thumb-sized piece ginger, cut into fine matchsticks

4 spring onions, cut into 3cm/1¼in lengths

200g/7oz pineapple, cut into chunks

handful coriander leaves, to garnish

boiled rice and steamed greens, to serve (optional)

**1** Mix the steak, soy sauce, sugar, chilli sauce and vinegar together in a large bowl, and set aside for 10 minutes.

**2** Heat a wok with 1 teaspoon of the oil. Lift the steak from the marinade and sear, in batches, then remove. Add a bit more oil and fry the ginger until golden. Add the spring onions and pineapple, and return the steak to the pan. Stir to heat through for 1 minute, then add any remaining marinade. Keep stirring until the marinade becomes thick and everything is hot. Serve sprinkled with coriander, along with rice and greens, if you like.

PER SERVING 267 kcals, protein 22g, carbs 18g, fat 12g, sat fat 5g, fibre 1g, sugar 18g, salt 2.4g

# Fish fingers & mushy peas

*A family favourite made special at home. Crispy fish fingers are easy to make yourself, and the children can help with the dipping and coating.*

**TAKES 25 MINUTES, PLUS CHILLING**
● **SERVES 4**

600g/1lb 5oz sustainable firm skinless white fish, such as pollack or hake
50g/2oz plain flour, seasoned
1 large egg, lightly whisked
200g/7oz fine fresh breadcrumbs
2 tbsp vegetable oil
400g/14oz frozen peas
knob butter
zest 1 lemon, then cut into wedges
small handful mint, finely shredded
steamed new potatoes, to serve (optional)

**1** Slice the fish into 12 fingers, each about 3cm/1¼in thick. Put the seasoned flour, egg and breadcrumbs into three separate shallow bowls. Dust the fish pieces first in the flour, then coat well in the egg and cover completely in the breadcrumbs. Put on a plate and chill for 15 minutes.

**2** Heat the oil in a large frying pan. Add the fish fingers and fry for 8 minutes, turning occasionally, until golden and cooked through. Meanwhile, add the peas to a small pan of boiling water. Cook for 4 minutes until really tender. Drain, tip into a bowl with the butter, zest and mint, and roughly mash with a potato masher. Season to taste and keep warm.

**3** Serve the golden fish fingers with a generous spoonful of mushy peas, the lemon wedges and some new potatoes, if you like.

PER SERVING 489 kcals, protein 42g, carbs 55g, fat 11g, sat fat 2g, fibre 9g, sugar 5g, salt 1.3g

# Sweet & sour pork stir-fry

*A home-cooked supper doesn't get much quicker than this – ready and on the table in just 15 minutes too.*

**TAKES 15 MINUTES • SERVES 2**

227g can pineapple slices in juice, drained and chopped, juice reserved

1 tbsp cornflour

1 tbsp tomato sauce

1 tsp soy sauce

1 tsp brown sugar

2½ tbsp rice wine vinegar or white wine vinegar

1 tbsp sunflower oil

200g/7oz stir-fry pork strips, trimmed of fat

1 red pepper, deseeded and cut into chunks

3 spring onions, quartered and shredded

boiled rice or noodles, to serve

**1** First, make the sauce by mixing 4 tablespoons of the pineapple juice into the cornflour until smooth, then stir in the tomato sauce, soy, sugar and vinegar. Set aside.

**2** Heat the oil in a wok until very hot, then throw in the pork for 1 minute, stirring. Lift the pork out on to a plate, then set aside.

**3** Add the pepper, stir-fry for around 2 minutes, then add the chopped pineapple and most of the spring onions for 30 seconds. Stir in the sauce for 1 minute, splashing in a little water as it cooks, then stir the pork back in for 20–30 seconds until just cooked through – it should still be tender. Scatter with the remaining spring onions and serve with rice or noodles.

PER SERVING 284 kcals, protein 24g, carbs 31g, fat 8g, sat fat 2g, fibre 2g, sugar 24g, salt 0.96g

# Chicken & mango stir-fry

*This is a great flavour combo. Choose a slightly under-ripe mango or it may go mushy. When time is short, a bag of ready-prepared stir-fry veg saves a lot of chopping time.*

**TAKES 30 MINUTES • SERVES 4**

450g/1lb boneless skinless chicken
  breasts
1 ripe mango
4 tbsp vegetable oil
1 bunch spring onions, diagonally sliced
small piece ginger, grated
1 garlic clove, crushed
350g bag fresh stir-fry vegetables
3 tbsp soy sauce
1 tbsp sweet chilli sauce
boiled rice or noodles, to serve

**1** Slice the chicken into thin strips. Cut the mango lengthways on either side of the stone, then peel off the skin and chop the flesh into cubes.

**2** Heat half the oil in a large frying pan or wok. Add the chicken and stir-fry for 4–5 minutes until lightly coloured. Remove from the pan with a slotted spoon and transfer to a plate. Heat the remaining oil in the pan and add the spring onions, ginger and garlic. Stir-fry for 30 seconds, then add the mango and vegetables, and stir-fry for a further 1 minute.

**3** Return the chicken to the pan and splash in the soy and chilli sauces. Stir until evenly mixed, then cover and cook for a further 2 minutes until the chicken is tender and the veggies are slightly softened. Serve with rice or noodles.

PER SERVING 201 kcals, protein 31g, carbs 16g, fat 2g, sat fat 1g, fibre 4g, sugar none, salt 2.48g

# Steamed fish & pak choi parcels

*Cooking the fish in parcels keeps the flesh moist and all the flavours sealed in – children love having their own parcel to open on their plates, too!*

**TAKES 25 MINUTES** ● **MAKES 4**

4 plaice, haddock or other sustainably
    sourced white fish fillets
2 pak choi, thickly sliced
4 spring onions, shredded
1 red chilli, deseeded and thinly sliced
3cm/1¼in piece ginger, cut into
    matchsticks
2 tbsp reduced-salt soy sauce
juice 1 lime
1 tsp sesame oil
boiled rice, to serve

**1** Heat oven to 200C/180C fan/gas 6. Put each fish fillet in the centre of a large square of foil. Top with the pak choi, spring onions, chilli and ginger, then pull up the edges of the foil.

**2** Mix together the soy sauce, lime juice and 1 tablespoon water then spoon a little over each fillet. Crimp the top of the foil to enclose the fish and make sure there are no gaps for the steam to escape.

**3** Put the parcels on a baking sheet and bake for 10–15 minutes until the fish is cooked through (this will depend on the thickness of your fish). Open up the parcels and drizzle over a few drops of sesame oil. Serve with rice.

PER PARCEL 124 kcals, protein 22g, carbs 2g, fat 3g, sat fat none, fibre 1g, sugar 2g, salt 1.31g

# Pork & noodle stir-fry

*The lime and coriander give this a really fresh Asian flavour. Add some chopped red chilli with the spring onions if you want to add a bit of a kick to this stir-fry.*

**TAKES 25 MINUTES, PLUS SOAKING**
• **SERVES 4**

200g/7oz thin rice noodles
400g pack lean minced pork
1 bunch spring onions, sliced into
  chunks
2 carrots, cut into matchsticks
5 tbsp soy sauce
1½ tbsp caster sugar
3 tbsp rice wine vinegar or white wine
  vinegar
juice 1 lime
handful mint and coriander leaves,
  roughly chopped

**1** Put the rice noodles in a bowl and pour over enough boiling water to cover. Cover the bowl with cling film and leave to soak for 10 minutes.

**2** Meanwhile, heat a large wok or frying pan and crumble in the mince. Dry-fry with some seasoning, breaking it up with a fork or wooden spoon for 7–10 minutes until browned. Throw in the spring onions and carrots, and cook for 2 minutes more.

**3** Mix together the soy sauce, sugar, vinegar and lime juice. Drain the noodles, add to the pan and heat through. Pour in the dressing, top with the herbs and serve.

PER SERVING 362 kcals, protein 28g, carbs 54g, fat 5g, sat fat 2g, fibre 2g, sugar 12g, salt 3.83g

# Smoked trout, beetroot & horseradish flatbread

*The lovely flavours of the smoked fish, creamy horseradish and earthy beetroot mingle together with the dill for this light lunch dish.*

**TAKES 20 MINUTES ● MAKES 4**

4 flatbreads
olive oil, for brushing
2 tbsp creamed horseradish
2 tbsp crème fraîche
small bunch dill, ½ chopped, ½ picked
  into small fronds
squeeze lemon juice, plus pinch zest
3 cooked beetroots (not in vinegar),
  very thinly sliced
4 smoked trout fillets, broken into large
  flakes
mixed salad leaves, to serve (optional)

**1** Heat oven to 220C/200C fan/gas 7. Brush the flatbreads with olive oil. Put on a large baking sheet and pop in the oven for about 8 minutes until crisp round the edges.

**2** Meanwhile, mix the horseradish, crème fraîche, chopped dill, lemon juice and zest, and some seasoning. Add a few drops of water to loosen the mixture to a drizzling consistency.

**3** Top each flatbread with some beetroot slices and smoked trout. Drizzle over the horseradish sauce, sprinkle with dill fronds and serve with salad, if you like.

PER FLATBREAD 327 kcals, protein 21g, carbs 42g, fat 10g, sat fat 4g, fibre 3g, sugar 5g, salt 2.1g

# Sweet & sour chicken with veg

*Upping the amount of veg and cutting down on the meat makes this a healthy alternative to a takeaway, and it is a good source of vitamin C too.*

**TAKES 40 MINUTES ● SERVES 4**

425g can pineapple chunks, drained, juice reserved

2 tbsp tomato ketchup

2 tbsp malt vinegar

2 tbsp cornflour

1 tbsp vegetable oil

1 onion, chopped

1 red chilli, deseeded and sliced

1 red and 1 green pepper, deseeded and chopped

2 carrots, sliced on the diagonal

2 boneless skinless chicken breasts, thinly sliced

125g pack baby corn, sliced lengthways

2 tomatoes, quartered

boiled rice, to serve (optional)

**1** Make the sauce by whisking together the pineapple juice, tomato ketchup, malt vinegar and cornflour. There should be 300ml/½ pint – add some water or stock if you're short.

**2** Heat the oil in a frying pan or wok over a high heat. Add the onion, chilli, peppers, carrots and chicken, and stir-fry for 3–5 minutes until the vegetables are starting to soften and the chicken is almost cooked.

**3** Add the corn and sauce. Bubble for 2 minutes, add the tomatoes and cook for 2 minutes until the sauce thickens, the chicken is cooked and the vegetables are tender. Serve with rice, if you like.

PER SERVING 230 kcals, protein 20g, carbs 30g, fat 4g, sat fat 1g, fibre 4g, sugar 24g, salt 0.26g

# Prawn chow mein

*This is really tasty with a lovely tang from the oyster sauce – good comfort food, with a lighter feel. If you have any leftover roast chicken, shred it and add with the prawns.*

**TAKES 25 MINUTES • SERVES 4**

3 nests medium egg noodles

140g/5oz broccoli, chopped into small
    florets

140g/5oz baby corn, halved

1 tbsp olive oil

1 red pepper, deseeded and sliced

300g/10oz cooked peeled prawns

**FOR THE SAUCE**

3 tbsp tomato ketchup

2 tbsp oyster sauce

**1** Cook the noodles, broccoli and corn in boiling water for 3–4 minutes, or until tender. Drain and set aside. Heat the oil in a large frying pan or wok and stir-fry the pepper for 3 minutes, until starting to soften.

**2** Tip in the noodles and vegetables along with the prawns and toss together. Add the sauce ingredients and heat everything through for 2–3 minutes, until piping hot.

PER SERVING 271 kcals, protein 25g, carbs 34g, fat 5g, sat fat 1g, fibre 5g, sugar 8g, salt 2.98g

# Clam, chorizo & white bean stew

*The spicy kick of Spanish chorizo works brilliantly with seafood here. Adding the white beans makes it a satisfying dish – perfect served simply with some crusty bread.*

**TAKES 35 MINUTES ● SERVES 2**

50g/2oz chorizo, diced
1 onion, finely chopped
1 garlic clove, crushed
small bunch flat-leaf parsley, ½ finely
  chopped, ½ roughly chopped
200ml/7fl oz hot stock, fish or
  vegetable
400g can chopped tomatoes
400g can butter beans or other white
  beans, drained and rinsed
1 tsp sherry vinegar
600g/1lb 5oz clams, cleaned
crusty bread, to serve

**1** Fry the chorizo in a large frying pan with a lid over a medium heat until it is starting to crisp up and release its oil. Add the onion and cook for 5 minutes until starting to soften. Then add the garlic and finely chopped parsley, and fry for 1 minute more.

**2** Pour on the stock and tomatoes. Bring to the boil, reduce the heat, then add the beans and sherry vinegar. Simmer for 10 minutes until the liquid is slightly reduced.

**3** Scatter over the clams, cover with the lid and steam for 2–4 minutes, shaking the pan occasionally until the clams are open (discard any clams that do not open). Have a little taste before seasoning, as the clams can be quite salty. Then scatter over the chopped parsley. Eat with lots of crusty bread.

PER SERVING 285 kcals, protein 28g, carbs 27g, fat 8g, sat fat 3g, fibre 9g, sugar 10g, salt 2.82g

# Thai-style fish broth with greens

*A lovely light lunch packed with Asian flavours. Pollack can be used in any recipe instead of cod or haddock and is usually cheaper.*

**TAKES 25 MINUTES • SERVES 2**

100g/4oz brown rice noodles
500ml/18fl oz chicken or fish stock
1 tbsp Thai red curry paste
4 dried or fresh kaffir lime leaves
1 tbsp Thai fish sauce
200g/7oz skinless sustainable white
    fish, such as pollack
100g/4oz raw peeled king prawns
2 pak choi, leaves separated
handful coriander leaves, to garnish

**1** Cook the noodles according to the pack instructions. Refresh in cold water and drain well then set aside.
**2** Put the stock in a large pan and stir in the curry paste, lime leaves, fish sauce and 250ml/8fl oz cold water. Bring to a simmer and cook for 5 minutes.
**3** Cut the fish into roughly 3cm/1¼in cubes and add to the pan. Return to a simmer, then cook for a further 2 minutes, uncovered.
**4** Stir in the noodles, prawns and pak choi, and simmer for 2–3 minutes or until the fish and prawns are just cooked. Serve in bowls scattered with coriander.

PER SERVING 330 kcals, protein 40g, carbs 35g, fat 4g, sat fat 1g, fibre 2g, sugar 1g, salt 2.9g

# Sweet & sour chicken skewers with fruity noodles

*Sweet–and–sour flavours are always popular with children, and noodles are a hit too, so this supper is sure to become a favourite in your house.*

**TAKES 30 MINUTES • SERVES 4**

425g can pineapple chunks, drained, juice reserved

4 tbsp tomato ketchup

2 tbsp white wine vinegar

6 boneless skinless chicken thighs, cut into chunks

2 red chillies, deseeded and chopped

1 red pepper, deseeded and cut into chunks

3 nests egg noodles

small bunch spring onions, sliced

**1** Mix the pineapple juice, tomato ketchup, vinegar and some seasoning together to make a sauce. Reserve half, then add the rest to a bowl with the chicken and half the red chilli. Set aside to marinate for 5 minutes.

**2** Thread the chicken, pepper and half the pineapple chunks on to eight skewers.

**3** Heat your grill, or fire up a barbecue. Brush any excess marinade from the chicken over the skewers, then grill or barbecue them, turning regularly, for about 8 minutes or until the chicken is starting to char at the edges and is cooked through.

**4** Meanwhile, cook the noodles according to the pack instructions, drain, then stir through the remaining pineapple, the rest of the chilli and the spring onions. Serve with the reserved sauce on the side or drizzled on top of the skewers.

PER SERVING 545 kcals, protein 44g, carbs 83g, fat 6g, sat fat 2g, fibre 4g, sugar 19g, salt 1.92g

# Full English frittata with smoky beans

*Looking for a new idea for Friday night's supper? Try this dish packed with all the family favourites. Or serve it up for a Sunday brunch – perfect!*

**TAKES 35 MINUTES • SERVES 4**

2 low-fat sausages, sliced

4 rashers extra-lean bacon, all fat removed, chopped

150g pack button mushrooms, halved, or larger ones quartered

8 egg whites or 350ml/12fl oz liquid egg whites from a carton

3 tbsp milk

140g/5oz cherry tomatoes, halved

2 × 400g cans reduced salt and sugar baked beans

1½ tsp smoked paprika

small bunch chives, snipped

**1** Heat oven to 180C/160C fan/gas 4. Line a roasting tin about the size of A4 paper with enough baking parchment to cover the base and sides. Fry the sausages and bacon in a non-stick pan until golden, stirring them often to stop them sticking. Scoop into the tin.

**2** Put the pan back on the heat and fry the mushrooms for about 5 minutes until golden, then add these to the tin, too. Whisk the egg whites with the milk and lots of seasoning. Pour into the tin, then dot the tomatoes on top.

**3** Bake in the oven for 20–25 minutes, until set. Meanwhile, tip the beans into a pan with the paprika and heat through. Scatter the frittata with the chives and serve with the beans on the side.

PER SERVING 268 kcals, protein 26g, carbs 27g, fat 6g, sat fat 2g, fibre 9g, sugar 7g, salt 3.3g

# Herby lamb burgers with beetroot mayo

*New flavour combinations like this traditional burger topped with beetroot mayo turn an old favourite into a fabulous modern combo to wake up the tastebuds.*

**TAKES 25 MINUTES • SERVES 4**

400g/14oz minced lamb
1 small red onion, ½ grated, ½ thinly
  sliced
handful parsley, roughly chopped
handful mint, roughly chopped
1 tsp olive oil
3 tbsp mayonnaise
2 cooked beetroot, finely chopped
4 bread rolls, halved
couple handfuls watercress

**1** Mix the lamb, grated onion and herbs in a bowl with some seasoning, then divide the mix into four and shape into burgers.

**2** Heat a griddle pan until hot, rub the burgers with oil and cook for 5–6 minutes on each side, or until cooked through.

**3** Meanwhile, mix the mayonnaise and beetroot with some seasoning. Fill the bread rolls with some watercress, a burger, a dollop of beetroot mayo and a few onion slices. Serve immediately.

PER SERVING 490 kcals, protein 25g, carbs 25g, fat 32g, sat fat 9g, fibre 2g, sugar 4g, salt 1.1g

# Garlic chilli prawns with sesame noodles

*On the table in just 20 minutes, this easy stir-fry includes the crisp crunch of beansprouts and is sure to become a family favourite.*

**TAKES 20 MINUTES • SERVES 4**

250g/9oz medium egg noodles
1 tbsp sesame oil, plus extra to drizzle (optional)
1 tbsp groundnut oil
1 bunch spring onions, thinly sliced lengthways
300g bag beansprouts
4 garlic cloves, finely chopped
1 red chilli, deseeded and finely chopped
400g/14oz raw peeled tiger prawns
1 tbsp soft brown sugar
1 tbsp dark soy sauce

**1** Cook the noodles according to the pack instructions, then rinse with cold water and drain. Toss with 1 teaspoon of the sesame oil.

**2** Heat 2 teaspoons of the groundnut oil in a non-stick wok. Stir-fry most of the spring onions and all the beansprouts for a couple of minutes until tender. Add the noodles and warm through. Stir through the remaining sesame oil and tip out of the wok on to a serving dish; keep warm.

**3** Carefully wipe out the wok and add the remaining groundnut oil. Toss in the garlic and chilli, and cook for 10 seconds. Pop in the prawns and stir-fry for a couple of minutes until they have just turned pink. Stir in the sugar and soy, then bubble until the sugar has melted and the prawns are cooked through. Spoon on top of the noodles and sprinkle with the remaining spring onions. Add an extra drizzle of sesame oil, if you like.

PER SERVING 430 kcals, protein 28g, carbs 51g, fat 13g, sat fat 3g, fibre 5g, sugar 9g, salt 1.5g

# Baked asparagus risotto

*Here's a risotto that doesn't need endless stirring on the hob as it's baked in the oven. Serve with some crusty bread and crisp green salad leaves.*

**TAKES 55 MINUTES • SERVES 4**

2 tsp olive oil
1 small onion, chopped
300g/10oz risotto rice
400ml can asparagus soup
850ml/1½ pints vegetable stock
small bunch parsley, chopped
300g/10oz asparagus, ends trimmed
10 cherry tomatoes, halved
25g/1oz Parmesan, grated

**1** Heat oven to 200C/180C fan/gas 6. Heat the oil in an ovenproof casserole dish with a lid, add the onion and cook for 5 minutes until softened. Add the rice and cook for 1 minute more, stirring to coat in the oil. Tip in the soup and stock, season and stir well to combine, then bring to the boil. Cover and put in the oven.

**2** Bake for 15 minutes, then remove the dish from the oven, give the rice a good mix, stirring in the parsley. Put the asparagus and tomatoes on top of the rice. Return to the oven, uncovered, for a further 15 minutes. Scatter with the cheese to serve.

PER SERVING 403 kcals, protein 12g, carbs 70g, fat 8g, sat fat 4g, fibre 4g, sugar 6g, salt 1.3g

# Zingy chicken stir-fry

*This recipe is easily doubled for a family or halved to serve one. Lemons can be used instead of the limes, if you prefer. The toasted sesame seeds add a good crunch.*

**TAKES 20 MINUTES • SERVES 2**

2 nests egg noodles
2 tsp sunflower oil
2 cooked chicken breasts, shredded
3 carrots, finely sliced
2 tbsp clear honey
1 tbsp soy sauce
juice 2 limes
3 tbsp toasted sesame seeds
handful coriander leaves, to garnish

**1** Cook the noodles according to the pack instructions, then drain and toss with 1 teaspoon of the oil.

**2** Heat the remaining oil in a wok and add the chicken and carrots. Stir-fry for a few minutes. Add the honey, soy and lime juice, bubble for 30 seconds, then add the noodles and sesame seeds. Mix well, heat through and sprinkle with coriander to serve.

PER SERVING 697 kcals, protein 51.2g, carbs 71g, fat 21.6g, sat fat 4g, fibre 8.4g, sugar 26.4g, salt 2.1g

# Jerk pork skewers with black beans & rice

*The pork and pineapple flavours really complement each other. Cook in a griddle pan or, if the sun shines, pop these skewers on the barbecue.*

**TAKES 20 MINUTES • SERVES 4**

400g/14oz pork fillet, cut into 4cm/1½in
   chunks

2 tbsp jerk or Creole seasoning

1 tsp ground allspice

1 tbsp hot chilli sauce, plus extra to
   serve (optional)

3 limes, zest and juice 1, other 2 cut
   into wedges to garnish

½ small pineapple, peeled, cored and
   cut into 4cm/1½in chunks

1 tbsp vegetable oil

200g/7oz basmati rice

400g can black beans, drained and
   rinsed

**1** Mix together the pork, jerk or Creole seasoning, allspice, chilli sauce, if using, lime zest and juice, and some seasoning. Thread the pork and pineapple on to metal skewers (or pre-soaked wooden skewers) and brush with the oil. Set aside.

**2** Cook the rice according to the pack instructions. Drain well, put back in the pan with the beans, then stir and keep warm.

**3** Meanwhile, heat a griddle pan until very hot. Cook the skewers for 3 minutes on each side until nicely charred and the pork is cooked through. Serve the skewers with the beans and rice, extra chilli sauce, if you like, and the lime wedges for squeezing over.

PER SERVING 451 kcals, protein 30g, carbs 57g, fat 10g, sat fat 3g, fibre 6g, sugar 7g, salt 0.2g

# Salmon & horseradish burgers

*These fish burgers are easy to make for a light summery lunch. Serve with some dill mayo and watercress on poppy seed rolls for finger food at its best.*

**TAKES 28 MINUTES • MAKES 4**

4 skinless salmon fillets or 1 large piece (about 500g/1lb 2oz) in total
1 tbsp creamed horseradish
zest 1 lemon and 2 tsp juice
small handful dill, chopped
1 tbsp vegetable oil
4 tbsp mayonnaise
4 poppy seed rolls, split
85g bag watercress
25g/1oz cucumber, sliced
4 radishes, thinly sliced

**1** Put the salmon, horseradish, lemon zest and half the dill in a food processor, then season and blitz to a fine paste.
**2** Shape the mixture into four burgers. Heat the oil in a large frying pan and cook the burgers for 4 minutes on each side until golden.
**3** Meanwhile, mix the remaining dill with the mayonnaise and spread a little on to the base of each roll. Toss the watercress in the lemon juice and put a handful on each roll base. Top with a burger and finish with slices of cucumber and radish. Replace the roll tops to serve, if you like, or serve them alongside.

PER BURGER 653 kcals, protein 32g, carbs 31g, fat 44g, sat fat 7g, fibre 3g, sugar 4g, salt 1.1g

# Watercress & chicken stir-fry

*Stir the watercress through at the last moment so it only wilts slightly and keeps its bright colour and satisfying crunch.*

**TAKES 25 MINUTES ● SERVES 4**

1 tbsp sunflower oil
2 boneless skinless chicken breasts, cut into strips
100g/4oz cashew nuts
1 yellow or red pepper, deseeded and chopped into large chunks
1 red onion, chopped into large chunks
2 × 75g bags watercress
boiled rice, to serve

**FOR THE SAUCE**

3 tbsp hoisin sauce
2 tbsp soy sauce
large piece ginger, finely grated
2 garlic cloves, crushed
1 tbsp sesame oil
2 tbsp rice wine vinegar or white wine vinegar

**1** To make the sauce, mix all the ingredients together in a small bowl until completely blended.

**2** Heat the oil in a frying pan until very hot. Throw in the chicken, cashew nuts, pepper and onion, then stir-fry for about 4–5 minutes until the chicken is cooked and the nuts are toasted. Pour over the sauce and simmer with a splash of water.

**3** Remove the pan from the heat, then stir through the watercress just before serving with boiled rice.

PER SERVING 323 kcals, protein 24g, carbs 15g, fat 19g, sat fat 2g, fibre 3g, sugar 10g, salt 1.92g

# Grilled salmon tacos with chipotle–lime yogurt

*Quick, enjoyable and bursting with delicious flavours, you can prepare everything beforehand then simply cook the salmon, warm the wraps and serve.*

**TAKES 25 MINUTES ● SERVES 4**

1 tsp garlic salt
2 tbsp smoked paprika
good pinch sugar
500g/1lb 2oz salmon fillet, skin on
200g/7oz fat-free yogurt
1 tbsp chipotle paste or hot chilli sauce
juice 1 lime

**TO SERVE**

8 small soft flour tortillas, warmed
¼ small green cabbage, finely shredded
small bunch coriander, picked into
    sprigs
few pickled jalapeño chillies, sliced
lime wedges, to garnish
hot chilli sauce, to drizzle (optional)

**1** Rub the garlic salt, paprika, sugar and some seasoning into the flesh of the salmon fillet. Heat grill to high.

**2** Mix the yogurt, chipotle paste or chilli sauce and lime juice together in a bowl with some seasoning, and set aside. Put the salmon on a baking sheet lined with foil and grill, skin-side down, for 7–8 minutes until cooked through. Remove from the grill and carefully peel off and discard the skin.

**3** Flake the salmon into large chunks and serve with the warmed tortillas, chipotle yogurt, shredded cabbage, coriander, jalapeños and lime wedges. Add a shake of hot chilli sauce, if you like it spicy.

---

PER SERVING 297 kcals, protein 33g, carbs 8g, fat 15g, sat fat 3g, fibre 5g, sugar 7g, salt 1.5g

# Roast pork with couscous & ginger yogurt

*Here's an updated Sunday lunch – the pork fillet is coated in spices before roasting and served with some fruity couscous and a ginger–yogurt dressing.*

**TAKES 50 MINUTES • SERVES 6**

2 pork fillets, each about 500g/1lb 2oz
   in total, trimmed of any fat
2 tsp olive oil
3 tsp ground cumin
1 tsp ground cinnamon
4 tsp grated ginger
250g/9oz couscous
100g/4oz sultanas
zest and juice 1 lemon
small bunch mint, chopped
200g/7oz fat-free natural yogurt

**1** Heat oven to 190C/170C fan/gas 5. Brown the pork in a non-stick frying pan over a high heat for 4–5 minutes, turning twice. Mix the oil, 2 teaspoons of the cumin, the cinnamon, 2 teaspoons of the ginger and some seasoning, then rub all over the pork. Transfer to a roasting tin and cook in the oven for 30–35 minutes or until the juices run clear when the thickest part is pierced with a skewer.
**2** Mix the couscous with the remaining cumin, the sultanas, lemon zest and juice, then season and pour over 400ml/14fl oz boiling water. Stir well and cover for 5 minutes, then stir in the mint.
**3** Stir the remaining ginger and a little seasoning into the yogurt. Thickly slice the pork and serve with the couscous and ginger yogurt.

PER SERVING 284 kcals, protein 23g, carbs 37g, fat 6g, sat fat 1g, fibre none, sugar 15g, salt 0.21g

# Rigatoni with spiced prawns, tomatoes & chorizo

*Fresh tomatoes work brilliantly here because the flavour of the prawns and chorizo is so big that you don't need a rich, intense tomato kick – more of a subtle, sweet taste.*

**TAKES 45 MINUTES** ● **SERVES 5–6**

4 tbsp olive oil

2 shallots, diced

120g/4½oz uncooked chorizo sausage, thinly sliced

6 large tomatoes, chopped

350g/12oz rigatoni

200g/7oz large raw prawns, shells and tails removed if necessary, chopped

2 large spring onions, thinly sliced, keep the whites and greens separate

**1** Put the oil, shallots and a grind of pepper in a large frying pan. Cook over a low heat for 10 minutes, stirring, until softened.

**2** Add the chorizo, turn up the heat (but not too much) and colour a little. When the orange oil is released, add the tomatoes and a pinch of salt. Stir over a medium heat – the tomatoes should melt in about 10 minutes. If the sauce is not bubbling, turn up the heat a little. Add 100ml/3½fl oz water and bring to the boil. Simmer for a few minutes more.

**3** Meanwhile, cook the pasta. Add the prawns to the sauce, bring back to the boil and cook for 1 minute until the prawns change colour. Drain the pasta and stir into the sauce with the white spring onion. Cook and stir for 1 minute. Serve sprinkled with the green spring onion.

PER SERVING (5) 462 kcals, protein 22g, carbs 60g, fat 17g, sat fat 4g, fibre 4g, sugar 8g, salt 1.14g

# Ratatouille with goat's cheese

*Ratatouille is a great way of getting a good portion of veg – and this dish includes four of your 5-a-day. This requires little effort as it's baked in the oven in one roasting tin.*

**TAKES 50 MINUTES** ● **SERVES 4**

1 red onion, cut into 8 wedges
1 medium aubergine, cut into bite-sized
    pieces
2 medium courgettes, thickly sliced
1 red and 1 yellow pepper, deseeded
    and chopped into bite-sized pieces
1 tbsp olive oil
400g can chopped tomatoes
handful basil leaves, roughly torn
100g/4oz goat's cheese, crumbled
crusty bread, jacket potato or pasta, to
    serve

**1** Heat oven to 200C/180C fan/gas 6. Put the onion, aubergine, courgettes and peppers in a roasting tin, and toss with the oil. Season and roast for 30 minutes until cooked.

**2** Stir in the tomatoes and basil, then scatter over the cheese. Return to the oven for 10 minutes more until bubbling and the cheese has melted. Serve hot with some crusty bread, in a jacket potato or over pasta.

PER SERVING 174 kcals, protein 10g, carbs 12g, fat 10g, sat fat 5g, fibre 5g, sugar 10g, salt 0.59g

# Caesar turkey burgers

*Make your own burgers, and they can be healthy! These are low in fat and salt, and give you two of your 5-a-day – a winner with all the family.*

**TAKES 35 MINUTES • MAKES 4**

1 garlic clove, crushed
1 anchovy, diced (optional)
juice 1 lemon
3 tbsp grated Parmesan
small bunch parsley, finely chopped
3 tbsp low-fat Greek yogurt
500g pack lean minced turkey
1 onion, finely chopped
1 Romaine lettuce, shredded
4 small wholemeal buns
2 tomatoes, sliced

**1** Heat oven to 200C/180C fan/gas 6. Mix together the garlic, anchovy, if using, lemon juice, two-thirds of the Parmesan and the parsley. Put half in a small bowl, mix with the yogurt and set aside. Mix the other half in a large bowl with the mince and onion, then season and shape into four burgers. Put the burgers in a roasting tin, then cook for 15–20 minutes until cooked through.

**2** Meanwhile, mix the lettuce with the yogurt dressing and slice the buns. To assemble, put the burgers in the buns with some lettuce and a few tomato slices. Serve the burgers with any leftover lettuce sprinkled with the reserved Parmesan.

PER BURGER 199 kcals, protein 12g, carbs 28g, fat 5g, sat fat 2g, fibre 4g, sugar 6g, salt 0.81g

# Coconut-crusted lime chicken

*Why not double the recipe, adding 8 chicken drumsticks instead of extra thighs, and that will be your family's lunchboxes sorted for the next day – brilliant!*

**TAKES 35 MINUTES • SERVES 4**

8 boneless skinless chicken thighs
zest and juice 2 limes, plus extra
    wedges to garnish
2 tsp medium curry powder or garam
    masala
1 tsp chilli powder (optional)
50g/2oz desiccated coconut
1 tbsp vegetable oil
mango chutney and boiled rice,
    to serve

**1** Heat oven to 200C/180C fan/gas 6. Put the chicken in a large bowl with the lime zest and juice, curry powder or garam masala, chilli powder, if using, and some seasoning. Mix well, then toss in the coconut to coat.

**2** Put the chicken on a wire rack sitting in a roasting tin, drizzle with the oil, then bake for 25 minutes until cooked through and tender. Serve with mango chutney, lime wedges for squeezing over and rice.

PER SERVING 316 kcals, protein 41g, carbs 2g, fat 16g, sat fat 9g, fibre 2g, sugar 1g, salt 0.49g

# Bolognese bake

*A jar of passata makes this a superquick spag-bol-turned-pasta-bake with a lovely cheesy crème-fraîche topping. This warm-you-up supper is a good budget-beater.*

**TAKES 25 MINUTES ● SERVES 6**

400g/14oz lean minced beef
3 garlic cloves, crushed
1 tbsp caster sugar
1 tbsp dried mixed Italian herbs
690ml jar passata with onions and garlic
350g/12oz penne
200ml tub half-fat crème fraîche
25g/1oz Parmesan, grated
salad and garlic bread, to serve

**1** In a large, non-stick frying pan, fry the mince until browned. Add the garlic, sugar and herbs, and cook for 1 minute more. Pour over the passata and add some seasoning, then simmer while you cook the pasta, according to the pack instructions.

**2** Heat grill to high. Mix the crème fraîche and Parmesan together. Spoon half the mince into an ovenproof dish. Mix the rest with the cooked, drained pasta and pour this on top. Drizzle over the Parmesan cream and grill until golden and bubbling. Serve with salad and garlic bread.

PER SERVING 449 kcals, protein 25g, carbs 54g, fat 15g, sat fat 7g, fibre 2g, sugar 9g, salt 0.85g

# Marinated bavette steak

*Cheaper cuts of steak have just as much flavour – if not more – than prime cuts. If you marinate them well before cooking, you'll get delicious steak at a fraction of the price.*

**TAKES 20 MINUTES, PLUS**
**MARINATING • SERVES 2**

2 × 250g/9oz bavette or flank steak
1 tbsp sunflower oil
1 rosemary sprig, bruised
mash or chips, to serve

**FOR THE MARINADE**

2 tbsp soy sauce
2 tbsp olive oil
2–3 garlic cloves
thumb-sized piece ginger, grated
juice ½ lemon, reserve lemon half
1 tbsp balsamic vinegar
1 tbsp clear honey

**1** For the marinade, mix all the ingredients together in a bowl. Put the steaks in a shallow dish and pour the marinade over to coat the meat completely. Cover, chill and leave to marinate overnight.

**2** Scrape the marinade off the steaks and rub each steak with a drop of sunflower oil. Heat a griddle pan until very hot, then rub the steaks with the reserved lemon half and cook with the rosemary sprig for 3–4 minutes each side, less for medium–rare, 1 minute longer if you prefer it cooked more. Rest for 5 minutes before serving with mash or chips.

PER SERVING 534 kcals, protein 57g, carbs 4g, fat 32g, sat fat 11g, fibre none, sugar 3g, salt 1.4g

# Grilled pork with lemon & thyme barley

*Barley makes a really good alternative to rice and couscous – it has a satisfying bite and is very filling.*

**TAKES 50 MINUTES ● SERVES 4**

4 pork medallions
2 tbsp red wine vinegar
2 garlic cloves, crushed
1 tbsp sunflower oil
1 small onion, finely chopped
1 tsp coriander seeds
200g/7oz pearl barley
600ml/1 pint hot chicken stock
4 lemon thyme sprigs, leaves only
100g bag baby leaf spinach
juice and zest 1 lemon

**1** Put the pork in a shallow non-metallic dish and add the vinegar and garlic, turning the meat pieces to make sure they are all evenly covered. Set aside at room temperature for 10 minutes.

**2** Meanwhile, heat the oil in a pan and cook the onion and coriander seeds for 3–4 minutes until softened. Add the barley and cook for 1 minute in the oil, then add the stock and thyme. Bring to the boil, cover, then simmer for 30–35 minutes until the barley is tender and the liquid absorbed.

**3** Transfer the pork to a grill pan and cook under a hot grill for 5 minutes on each side until nicely browned and cooked through. Stir the spinach, lemon zest and juice into the barley and spoon on to plates. Serve with the grilled pork.

PER SERVING 425 kcals, protein 37g, carbs 44g, fat 12g, sat fat 3g, fibre 1g, sugar 2g, salt 0.65g

# Peppered fillet steak with parsley potatoes

*Spoil yourselves with a mouthwatering prime cut of steak. Ring the changes by adding a little garlic and parsley to the accompanying sauté potatoes.*

**TAKES 40 MINUTES • SERVES 2**

3 large red-skinned potatoes, peeled and cut into large cubes
2 tbsp olive oil, plus a drizzle extra
1 garlic clove, minced
small bunch flat-leaf parsley, finely chopped
sea salt, to season
2 beef fillet steaks (about 140g/5oz each)
1 tsp cracked black pepper
small knob butter
watercress salad, to serve

**1** Tip the potatoes into a pan of water, bring to the boil, simmer for 2 minutes, then drain. Heat the oil in a non-stick frying pan. Add the potatoes and sizzle gently for 20 minutes, tossing occasionally, until golden and crispy all over. When the potatoes are cooked, add the garlic to the pan and fry for 1 minute more. Finally, toss through the parsley, season with sea salt and set aside.

**2** Meanwhile, rub the steaks with a drizzle of oil, then press in the black pepper. Heat a griddle pan until hot, and cook the steaks to your liking (2½ minutes each side for medium–rare, 3½ minutes for medium, 4½ minutes for well done). Leave the steaks to rest for 5 minutes, then top with a knob of butter and serve with the potatoes and some watercress salad.

PER SERVING 494 kcals, protein 35g, carbs 6g, fat 22g, sat fat 7g, fibre 4g, sugar 3g, salt 0.2g

# Polenta tart with sausage & broccoli

*Polenta, a yellow cornmeal, is an Italian favourite and a really versatile ingredient. Keep some in your cupboard for a Mediterranean alternative to mash or pastry.*

**TAKES 40 MINUTES • SERVES 4**

1 litre/1¾ pints vegetable stock
200g/7oz instant polenta
50g/2oz Parmesan, grated
140g/5oz thin-stemmed broccoli
200g/7oz ready-grated mozzarella
100g/4oz semi-dried tomatoes
1 garlic clove, chopped
4 Italian pork sausages, skins removed
  and meat split into bite-sized chunks

**1** Heat oven to 190C/170C fan/gas 5. In a large pan, bring the stock to the boil. Slowly pour in the polenta, a little at a time, stirring it as you do so until completely absorbed. Lower the heat, stir quickly for 5 minutes, then remove from the heat altogether. Stir in 1 tablespoon of the Parmesan, then gently spread the polenta out on a large parchment-lined baking sheet, so that the polenta is in an even layer 2–3cm/1–1¼in thick.

**2** Cook the broccoli in a pan of boiling salted water for 2 minutes, drain, then rinse under cold water.

**3** Sprinkle the mozzarella and remaining Parmesan over the polenta, then top with the tomatoes, garlic, broccoli and sausage chunks. Bake for 20 minutes until the sausage is browned and the sides of the polenta are crisp. Serve straight away.

PER SERVING 703 kcals, protein 29g, carbs 44g, fat 45g, sat fat 17g, fibre 3g, sugar 4g, salt 3.2g

# Pasta with pine nuts, broccoli, sardines & fennel

*This robust-and-gutsy flavour combination is very typically Sicilian. The raisins are sweet, the olive oil spicy, the pine nuts crunchy and the sardines salty.*

**TAKES 30 MINUTES • SERVES 6**

4 tbsp extra virgin olive oil, plus a splash

500g/1lb 2oz bucatini or long pasta, such as spaghetti

500g/1lb 2oz purple sprouting broccoli, stalks halved if very large

2 red onions, sliced

4 garlic cloves, thinly sliced

1 small fennel bulb, very thinly sliced

50g/2oz salted sardines or good-quality canned sardines in oil

25g/1oz pine nuts

25g/1oz raisins

juice and zest ½ lemon

chilli flakes, to garnish

**1** Bring a large pan of water to the boil, with a splash of the oil, then add the pasta. Cook according to the pack instructions, adding the broccoli for the final 5 minutes.

**2** Meanwhile, gently heat the remaining oil in a large pan. Add the onions and sliced garlic, and cook slowly for 2 minutes. Add the fennel and cook for a couple more minutes, until softened. Flake the sardines into the pan and stir around for a few more minutes to break them up.

**3** Tip the drained pasta and broccoli into the pan with the pine nuts, raisins and lemon juice. Toss together to let the pasta absorb the oil, then season well. Serve the pasta immediately, scattered with lemon zest and chilli flakes.

PER SERVING 462 kcals, protein 18g, carbs 67g, fat 13g, sat fat 2g, fibre 7g, sugar 10g, salt 0.1g

# Fisherman's curry

*A wonderful, light tomato-based curry from Kerala. Look out for fresh curry leaves when you're out shopping; if you buy a bunch, you can freeze any you don't use.*

**TAKES 45 MINUTES • SERVES 6**

juice 1 lemon

750g/1lb 10oz boneless skinless firm white fish, cut into large pieces

1 tbsp vegetable oil

1 cinnamon stick

4 whole cloves

4 green cardamom pods

½ tsp whole black peppercorns

10 fresh curry leaves

2 onions, chopped

3 green chillies, deseeded and finely chopped

1 tbsp grated ginger

4 garlic cloves, finely chopped

6 tomatoes, chopped, or 400g can chopped tomatoes

1 tsp turmeric powder

½ tsp chilli powder

2 tsp ground coriander

boiled rice, to serve

**1** Stir the lemon juice and 1 teaspoon salt into the fish pieces and set aside. Heat the oil in a large pan. Add the whole spices and curry leaves, cook for 3–4 minutes, then add the onions. Fry until the onions are soft, then add the chillies, ginger and garlic. Tip in the tomatoes and the remaining spices, and cook, uncovered, on a low heat for about 5–8 minutes. Stir frequently to prevent the spices sticking and burning.

**2** Pour 150ml/¼ pint water into the pan, bring to a simmer, then add the fish. Cover with a lid and cook for 5 minutes more. Serve with rice.

PER SERVING 152 kcals, protein 25g, carbs 7g, fat 3g, sat fat none, fibre 1g, sugar 4g, salt 1.1g

# Pad Thai with prawns

*Tamarind adds a distinctive sweet–sour flavour to dishes and is easiest to use as a paste. You can use any kind of noodles here – whatever you have in the cupboard.*

**TAKES 20 MINUTES • SERVES 2**

250g/9oz udon noodles
2 tsp vegetable oil
100g/4oz peeled raw prawns
4 spring onions, chopped
2 eggs, beaten
2 tbsp roasted peanuts, chopped, and
   small handful coriander leaves,
   to garnish
lime wedges, to squeeze over

**FOR THE SAUCE**

2 tbsp tamarind paste
1 tbsp Thai fish sauce
juice 1 lime
1 tbsp soft brown sugar

**1**  Boil the noodles in a pan of salted water for 3 minutes until soft. Drain and rinse in cold water.

**2**  To make the sauce, mix all the ingredients together in a small bowl.

**3**  Heat a wok with half the oil. Add the prawns and spring onions, and cook, stirring quickly, for 1 minute or until the prawns turn pink. Push the prawns to the side and add the remaining oil. Add the eggs and let sit for 30 seconds, then scramble until cooked. Add the noodles and sauce, and cook, stirring continuously, for 3 minutes or until everything is hot.

**4**  Serve the noodles with the peanuts and coriander sprinkled on top, and lime wedges for squeezing over.

PER SERVING 498 kcals, protein 27g, carbs 56g, fat 18g, sat fat 3g, fibre 4g, sugar 22g, salt 2.3g

# Greek beans with seared lamb

*Cook the lamb to your liking then leave it to rest before slicing for the juiciest result.*
*The tomatoey beans and feta add a real taste of the Med to this meat dish.*

**TAKES 35 MINUTES • SERVES 4**

500g/1lb 2oz lamb fillet
1½ tbsp olive oil
3 garlic cloves, crushed
1 large onion, chopped
2 tbsp tomato purée
small bunch dill, most chopped, some
    leaves left to garnish
1 tbsp red wine vinegar
500ml/18fl oz chicken stock
2 × 400g cans gigante or butter beans,
    drained and rinsed
2 tbsp crumbled feta

**1** Rub the lamb with ½ tablespoon of the oil and 1 garlic clove. Season well and set aside to marinate while you prepare the beans, or for up to 2 hours if you have time.

**2** Heat the remaining oil in a pan. Add the onion and remaining garlic, and season. Fry for 8 minutes until soft. Add the tomato purée, chopped dill, vinegar, stock and beans, season, and simmer for 15 minutes or until most of the liquid has evaporated.

**3** Meanwhile, heat a frying pan until hot. Sear the lamb on all sides, for about 5 minutes in total. Set aside to rest, covered with foil, for 5 minutes, then thickly slice. Serve the lamb with the beans, scattered with feta and the remaining dill leaves.

PER SERVING 437 kcals, protein 34g, carbs 22g, fat 24g, sat fat 9g, fibre 8g, sugar 6g, salt 0.8g

# Beef stir-fry with ginger

*A lovely dish for a dinner to celebrate Chinese New Year. Chinese five-spice is made of cinnamon, fennel, star anise, ginger and clove, and adds an aromatic flavour to dishes.*

**TAKES 30 MINUTES ● SERVES 4**

500g/1lb 2oz beef rump, trimmed and cut into thin strips

1 tsp Chinese five-spice

300g pack ready-cooked rice noodles

1 large red chilli, deseeded and thinly sliced

1 fat garlic clove, chopped

4cm/1½in piece ginger, cut into matchsticks

1 lemongrass stalk, trimmed and sliced

2 tbsp sunflower oil

100g/4oz sugar snaps, cut into thin strips

8 baby corn, sliced diagonally

6 spring onions, trimmed and sliced diagonally

juice ½ lime

2 tbsp soy sauce

1 tbsp Thai fish sauce

2 tbsp roasted peanuts, chopped

coriander leaves, to garnish

**1** Mix the beef and five-spice in a bowl, then set aside to marinate. Soften the noodles in boiling water according to the pack instructions, drain, then set aside. Mix the chilli with the garlic, ginger and lemongrass in a small bowl. Heat half the oil in a wok, add the chilli mixture and stir-fry for 1 minute until softened but not coloured. Remove with a slotted spoon and set aside.

**2** Heat the remaining oil, add the beef and stir-fry over a high heat for 1 minute until browned and just cooked through.

**3** Return the chilli mixture to the pan with the sugar snaps, corn and half the onions. Stir-fry for 1 minute more then add the drained noodles. Mix thoroughly to combine, take off the heat and add a squeeze of lime juice, the soy and fish sauces. Divide among four plates. Scatter with the peanuts, garnish with the remaining onions and the coriander.

PER SERVING 349 kcals, protein 33g, carbs 26g, fat 14g, sat fat 3g, fibre 1g, sugar 3g, salt 3.58g

# Mexican rice with chipotle pork & avocado salsa

*The spiciness of this pork works well with the rice and beans and avocado salsa, making a fabulous supper for two that is on the table in half an hour.*

**TAKES 30 MINUTES** • **SERVES 2**

400g/14oz pork shoulder steaks, cut into 3cm/1¼in pieces
2 tbsp chipotle paste
2 tsp ground cumin
2 tsp smoked paprika
1 tsp sugar
1 tsp vegetable oil
100g/4oz basmati rice
400g can black beans, drained and rinsed
1 avocado, cut into chunks
1 small red onion, finely chopped
handful coriander, roughly chopped
1 lime, ½ juiced, ½ cut into wedges
2 tbsp pickled jalapeño slices, rinsed

**1** Heat oven to 180C/160C fan/gas 4. Toss the pork with 1 tablespoon of the chipotle paste, the cumin, paprika, sugar and some seasoning. Spread on a baking sheet, drizzle with the oil and bake for 20 minutes until tender.

**2** Meanwhile, cook the rice according to the pack instructions until just cooked, then drain. Put back in the pan, add the beans and keep warm with a lid on.

**3** In a small bowl, toss the avocado with the red onion, most of the coriander, the remaining chipotle paste and the lime juice, then season. Serve the rice and beans with the pork, avocado salsa, jalapeño slices, lime wedges and remaining coriander.

PER SERVING 687 kcals, protein 54g, carbs 66g, fat 22g, sat fat 6g, fibre 11g, sugar 6g, salt 1.2g

# Basque-style salmon stew

*The veg included here means this healthy dish provides three of your 5-a-day, plus it's a good source of omega-3 and vitamin C.*

**TAKES 35 MINUTES • SERVES 4**

1 tbsp olive oil

3 mixed peppers, deseeded and sliced

1 large onion, thinly sliced

400g/14oz baby potatoes, unpeeled and halved

2 tsp smoked paprika

2 garlic cloves, sliced

2 tsp dried thyme

400g can chopped tomatoes

4 salmon fillets, skin on

1 tbsp chopped parsley, to garnish (optional)

**1** Heat the oil in a large pan and add the peppers, onion and potatoes. Cook, stirring regularly, for 5–8 minutes until golden. Then add the paprika, garlic, thyme and tomatoes. Bring to the boil, stir and cover, then turn down the heat and simmer for 12 minutes. Add a splash of water if the sauce becomes too thick.

**2** Season the stew and lay the salmon on top, skin-side down. Put the lid back on and simmer for another 8 minutes until the salmon is cooked right through. Scatter with parsley, if you like, and serve.

PER SERVING 414 kcals, protein 33g, carbs 29g, fat 19g, sat fat 4g, fibre 5g, sugar 11g, salt 0.33g

# Greek lamb traybake

*All cooked in one dish, this supper can be put together and left to cook while you get on with something else. For a lower-fat version, use turkey mince.*

**TAKES 55 MINUTES • SERVES 4**

50g/2oz fresh white breadcrumbs
250g/9oz minced lamb
1 egg, beaten
2 onions, halved
large handful mint, chopped
2 large potatoes, cut into wedges
2 courgettes, cut into batons
12 cherry tomatoes
2 tbsp olive oil
50g/2oz feta, crumbled
crusty bread, to serve

**1** Heat oven to 200C/180C fan/gas 6. Pop the breadcrumbs, lamb mince, egg and plenty of seasoning in a bowl. Grate in half an onion and sprinkle in half the chopped mint. Give everything a good mix and shape into eight patties. Put on a large, shallow roasting tin.

**2** Cut the remaining onion halves into wedges. Put them in the tin around the lamb patties with the potatoes, courgettes and cherry tomatoes. Drizzle with olive oil and season. Bake for around 40 minutes, turning everything once, until the lamb is cooked through and the vegetables are tender. Remove from the oven, sprinkle with the feta and remaining mint and serve with some crusty bread.

PER SERVING 388 kcals, protein 22g, carbs 35g, fat 19g, sat fat 7g, fibre 3g, sugar 7g, salt 0.77g

# Thai green chicken curry

*Don't let this green curry carry on cooking once the chicken is ready, otherwise you'll lose its fresh vibrant colour and spicy hot flavour.*

**TAKES 55 MINUTES • SERVES 4**

2 × 400g cans coconut milk

4 tbsp Thai green curry paste or to taste

800g/1lb 12oz boneless skinless chicken thighs, each thigh cut into three

6 lime leaves, stalks removed, shredded

3 lemongrass stalks, outer leaves removed and inner stalk finely chopped

25g/1oz galangal, sliced

1 tbsp palm sugar or light muscovado sugar

1 tbsp Thai fish sauce

handful pea aubergines or ½ aubergine, diced

small bunch Thai basil, leaves only, to garnish

boiled jasmine rice, to serve

**1** Scrape the thick, fatty part of the coconut milk into a warm wok. Cook it slowly, stirring all the time, until it starts to bubble and sizzle, and just begins to split. Add the green curry paste and cook for 3–4 minutes until the paste starts to release its fragrant aroma.

**2** Add the chicken and stir well, coating it all in the paste. Add the rest of the coconut milk, the lime leaves, lemongrass, galangal, palm or muscovado sugar and half the fish sauce. Let the sauce bubble for about 10 minutes, until the oil in the coconut milk starts to come through to the surface and the chicken is cooked. Add the aubergine and the rest of the fish sauce, and cook for 5 minutes more. Scatter over the Thai basil and serve with some jasmine rice.

PER SERVING 623 kcals, protein 46g, carbs 15g, fat 42g, sat fat 31g, fibre 3g, sugar 8g, salt 1.7g

# Italian sausage & pasta pot

*This is a fantastic one-pot meal that is packed with flavour, as the stock is enriched with all the ingredients that are cooked in it.*

**TAKES 35 MINUTES ● SERVES 4**

1 tbsp olive oil
8 Italian sausages
2.8 litres/5 pints hot chicken stock
400g/14oz penne
2 carrots, thinly sliced
2 onions, thinly sliced
3 celery sticks, thinly sliced
140g/5oz green beans, cut into
    5cm/2in lengths
handful flat-leaf parsley, chopped

**1** Heat the oil in a large pan and fry the sausages until brown all over. Pour in the hot chicken stock and simmer with a lid on for 10 minutes.

**2** Add the pasta to the pan, mix well and bring to the boil. Stir in the carrots and onions, cook for 5 minutes, then add the celery and beans, and cook for a further 4 minutes. Check that the pasta is cooked – if not, cook for a few minutes longer. Finally, stir in chopped parsley, season and serve in large bowls.

PER SERVING 772 kcals, protein 53g, carbs 90g, fat 25g, sat fat 8g, fibre 9g, sugar 11g, salt 3g

# Kung po prawns

*A quick homemade version of a takeaway classic. The prawns are butterflied here as it helps them to cook more quickly and trap the delicious sauce, but it's not essential.*

**TAKES 20 MINUTES ● SERVES 4**

400g/14oz large raw prawns (frozen are fine)
1 tsp cornflour
2 tbsp light soy sauce
2 tbsp Chinese rice vinegar
1 heaped tbsp tomato purée
1 tsp caster sugar
2 tbsp sunflower or groundnut oil
85g/3oz unsalted roasted peanuts
6 small or 3 large whole dried red chillies
2 × 225g cans water chestnuts, drained
thumb-sized piece ginger, finely grated
2 garlic cloves, finely chopped
boiled rice, to serve

**1** To butterfly a prawn, make a cut along its length, cutting almost all the way through. Pull out the black vein.

**2** Mix the cornflour and 1 tablespoon of the soy sauce together, toss in the prawns and set aside for 10 minutes. Stir the vinegar, remaining soy sauce, tomato purée, sugar and 2 tablespoons water together to make a sauce.

**3** Heat a large frying pan or wok until very hot, then add 1 tablespoon of the oil. Fry the prawns until they are golden in places and have opened out – then tip them out of the pan.

**4** Heat the remaining oil and add the peanuts, chillies and water chestnuts. Stir-fry for 2 minutes or until the peanuts start to colour, then add the ginger and garlic, and fry for 1 minute. Tip in the prawns and sauce, and simmer for 2 minutes until thickened slightly. Serve with rice.

PER SERVING 308 kcals, protein 25g, carbs 13g, fat 18g, sat fat 3g, fibre 1g, sugar 6g, salt 2.07g

# Moroccan chicken with sweet potato mash

*Ras-el-hanout, a North African spice mix, adds a spicy, herbal and floral flavour to dishes. You can find it in larger supermarkets.*

**TAKES 35 MINUTES • SERVES 4**

1kg/2lb 4oz sweet potatoes, cubed

2 tsp ras-el-hanout or a mix of ground cinnamon and cumin

4 boneless skinless chicken breasts

2 tbsp olive oil

1 onion, thinly sliced

1 fat garlic clove, crushed

200ml/7fl oz chicken stock

2 tsp clear honey

juice ½ lemon

handful green olives, pitted or whole

20g pack coriander, leaves chopped

**1** Boil the potatoes in salted water for 15 minutes or until tender. Mix the ras-el-hanout with some seasoning, then sprinkle it all over the chicken. Heat 1 tablespoon of the oil in a large frying pan, then brown the chicken for 3 minutes on each side until golden.

**2** Lift the chicken out of the pan. Add the onion and garlic, and cook for 5 minutes until softened. Add the stock, honey, lemon juice and olives, return the chicken to the pan, then simmer for 10 minutes until the sauce is syrupy and the chicken cooked.

**3** Mash the potatoes with the remaining tablespoon of oil and season. Thickly slice each chicken breast and stir the coriander through the sauce. Serve the chicken and sauce over the mash.

PER SERVING 460 kcals, protein 39g, carbs 59g, fat 9g, sat fat 2g, fibre 7g, sugar 18g, salt 1.11g

# Prawn & broccoli Asian omelette

*Here's a new way to serve an omelette, with the filling cooked briefly first and then rolled up inside the omelette. So easy – and ideal for teenagers to cook themselves.*

**TAKES 22 MINUTES • SERVES 2**

4 eggs, beaten
juice ½ lemon
sunflower oil, for frying
large handful small broccoli florets
200g/7oz large peeled cooked prawns
1 red chilli, chopped
1 large garlic clove, chopped
oyster sauce, to drizzle (optional)

**1** Beat the eggs and lemon juice together, and set aside.

**2** Heat 1 tablespoon of oil in a frying pan. Add the broccoli and stir-fry for 2 minutes. Add the prawns, chilli and garlic, and cook until the broccoli is just done. Tip everything out on to a plate and give the pan a wipe.

**3** Heat a drop more oil in the pan. Pour in half the egg mix and swirl it around to make a thin omelette. Flip over to cook the other side, then lift on to a serving plate and keep warm. Quickly make another omelette. Add half the prawn mix to each, roll up and serve drizzled with some oyster sauce, if you like.

PER SERVING 386 kcals, protein 39g, carbs 1g, fat 25g, sat fat 5g, fibre 1g, sugar 1g, salt 2.21g

# Thai satay stir-fry

*When stir-frying, if your vegetables aren't cooking as quickly as you'd like, add a splash of water to the pan. This creates a shot of steam and helps them to cook quicker.*

**TAKES 15 MINUTES • SERVES 4**

3 tbsp crunchy peanut butter
3 tbsp sweet chilli sauce
2 tbsp soy sauce
300g pack straight-to-wok noodles
1 tbsp sunflower oil
thumb-sized piece ginger, grated
300g pack stir-fry vegetables with peppers, mangetout and baby leaves
handful basil leaves
25g/1oz roasted peanuts, roughly chopped

**1** Mix the peanut butter, chilli sauce, 100ml/3½fl oz water and soy sauce to make a smooth satay sauce. Put the noodles in a bowl and pour boiling water over them. Stir gently to separate, then drain thoroughly.

**2** Heat the oil in a wok, then stir-fry the ginger and harder pieces of veg from the stir-fry mix, such as peppers, for 2 minutes. Add the noodles and rest of the veg, then stir-fry over a high heat for 1–2 minutes until the veg are just cooked.

**3** Push the veg to one side of the pan, then pour the peanut sauce into the other side, tilting the pan. Bring to the boil. Mix the sauce with the stir-fry, then sprinkle over the basil leaves and peanuts to serve.

PER SERVING 286 kcals, protein 10g, carbs 34g, fat 14g, sat fat 2g, fibre 5g, sugar 6g, salt 2.29g

# Indonesian fried rice with mackerel

*Great for midweek as supper is on the table in 20 minutes. Peppered mackerel fillets would also be good in this recipe.*

**TAKES 20 MINUTES • SERVES 4**

1 tbsp olive oil

2 eggs, lightly beaten

1 tbsp Thai red curry paste

pinch caster sugar

800g/1lb 12oz cooked basmati rice
(about 200g–300g/7oz–10oz
uncooked)

small bunch spring onions, sliced

140g/5oz frozen peas

2 tbsp soy sauce, plus extra to drizzle
(optional)

4 smoked mackerel fillets, flaked

½ cucumber, cut into half moons

**1** Heat the oil in a large frying pan or wok. Tip in the eggs and swirl to coat the base of the pan. Cook for 1 minute, then flip and cook the other side until set. Remove and roughly chop into ribbons.

**2** Add the curry paste and sugar to the pan and fry for 1 minute. Tip in the cooked rice and stir to coat in the paste, then add the spring onions and peas. Stir-fry for 2–3 minutes until everything is really hot. Add the soy sauce, then gently toss through the omelette ribbons and mackerel.

**3** Divide among four bowls and garnish with the cucumber. Serve with extra soy sauce, if you like.

PER SERVING 760 kcals, protein 34g, carbs 61g, fat 44g, sat fat 10g, fibre 4g, sugar 4g, salt 5.66g

# Easy paella

*Paella rice is similar to risotto rice and has a slightly chewy texture. This dish can easily be doubled for a get-together with friends.*

**TAKES 40 MINUTES • SERVES 4**

1 tbsp olive oil
1 onion, chopped
1 tsp hot smoked paprika
1 tsp dried thyme
300g/10oz paella or risotto rice
3 tbsp dry sherry or white wine (optional)
400g can chopped tomatoes with garlic
900ml/1½ pints chicken stock
400g bag frozen mixed seafood
juice ½ lemon, other ½ cut into wedges, to serve
handful flat-leaf parsley, roughly chopped

**1** Heat the oil in a large frying pan. Add the onion and soften for 5 minutes. Stir in the paprika, thyme and rice, stir for 1 minute, then splash in the sherry or wine, if using. Once it has evaporated, stir in the tomatoes and stock. Season and cook, uncovered, for about 15 minutes, stirring now and again until the rice is almost tender and still surrounded by some liquid.

**2** Stir the frozen seafood into the pan and cover with a lid. Simmer for 5 minutes, or until the seafood is cooked through and the rice is tender. Squeeze over the lemon juice, scatter with parsley and serve with the extra lemon wedges.

PER SERVING 431 kcals, protein 34g, carbs 66g, fat 5g, sat fat 1g, fibre 3g, sugar 5g, salt 2.14g

# Moroccan turkey meatballs with citrus couscous

*Serving spicy meatballs with orange-and-coriander couscous turns them into a healthy supper that's ready in half an hour. The spices add an authentic Moroccan flavour.*

**TAKES 30 MINUTES • SERVES 4**

500g pack minced turkey
2 tsp chilli powder
2 tsp ground cumin
2 tsp ground coriander
1 tsp ground cinnamon
1 onion, coarsely grated
zest 1 orange, peeled segments
    chopped
250g/9oz couscous
250ml/9fl oz hot chicken stock
2 tsp olive oil
small bunch coriander, roughly
    chopped

**1** In a big bowl, mix the mince, spices, onion and orange zest together really well with your hands. Roll the mixture into about 20 walnut-sized meatballs.
**2** Put the couscous in a bowl, pour over the hot chicken stock, cover with cling film and leave to stand for 10 minutes.
**3** Heat the olive oil in a frying pan. Add the meatballs and fry, turning often, for about 12 minutes until browned all over and cooked through.
**4** Fluff up the couscous with a fork, stir in the chopped orange segments, coriander and some seasoning. Pile on to plates and serve with the meatballs.

PER SERVING 348 kcals, protein 36g, carbs 41g, fat 6g, sat fat 1g, fibre 1g, sugar 6g, salt 0.45g

# Chocolate & banana French toast

*This is an indulgence for when you're feeling in the need of a quick chocolate fix. If you prefer, you could use dark chocolate to make it less sweet.*

**TAKES 18 MINUTES • SERVES 2**

1 ripe banana
75g/2½oz milk chocolate, chopped
4 slices crusty white bread from a
    round loaf
3 medium eggs
1 tbsp double cream
1 tbsp maple syrup
1 tsp vanilla extract
25g/1oz unsalted butter
ground cinnamon, to sprinkle
icing sugar or extra maple syrup, to
    dust or drizzle (optional)

**1**  Mash the banana in a small bowl using a fork. Add the chocolate and mix to combine.

**2**  Lay two slices of the bread on the work surface. Divide the chocolate-and-banana mixture between them, spreading it almost to the edges. Top each with a second slice of bread and press together to make a sandwich.

**3**  In a shallow dish, whisk together the eggs, cream, syrup and vanilla. Melt the butter in a large frying pan over a medium heat. Lay one sandwich in the egg mixture to coat one side, then carefully flip it over so that both sides of the sandwich are soaked in egg. Lower the sandwich into the hot frying pan and cook for 1 minute on each side, until golden and the chocolate has started to melt. Repeat with the second sandwich. Halve the sandwiches and sprinkle with cinnamon and either icing sugar or maple syrup.

PER SERVING 648 kcals, protein 16g, carbs 59g, fat 38g, sat fat 21g, fibre 2g, sugar 38g, salt 0.9g

# Rhubarb & ginger syllabub

*A classic syllabub is made with cream, so it's not the healthiest of puds. To reduce the fat content, simply swap the cream for natural yogurt.*

**TAKES 25 MINUTES • MAKES 4**

400g/14oz rhubarb, cut into small
cubes
thumb-sized piece ginger, finely
chopped
75g/2½oz caster sugar
100ml/3½fl oz white wine
100g/4oz light mascarpone
300ml/½ pint double cream
50g/2oz icing sugar
2 pieces crystallised ginger, finely
chopped

**1** Put the rhubarb, chopped root ginger, sugar and white wine in a pan, bring to the boil and simmer on a low heat for 4–5 minutes until the rhubarb has softened. Remove from the heat and set aside to cool.

**2** In a bowl, whisk the mascarpone, double cream and icing sugar to soft peaks. Remove 4 tablespoons of the cooled rhubarb and mash with a fork, then fold into the cream mixture.

**3** Divide the rest of the poached rhubarb among four glasses, reserving a bit. Spoon over the cream mixture, then top with a few pieces of crystallised ginger and the reserved rhubarb. This can be chilled for several hours before serving.

PER SYLLABUB 592 kcals, protein 5g, carbs 36g, fat 46g, sat fat 29g, fibre 1g, sugar 36g, salt 0.1g

# Grilled summer-berry pudding

*This recipe has the elements of a classic summer pudding but is much simpler to prepare and is served hot.*

**TAKES 30 MINUTES** • **SERVES 4**

4 slices white bread, crusts removed
85g/3oz golden caster sugar
2 tsp cornflour
200g tub low-fat fromage frais
300g/10oz mixed summer berries (we used raspberries, blueberries, redcurrants, sliced strawberries) or 300g/10oz frozen berries, defrosted

**1** Heat the grill to high. Lay the slices of bread slightly overlapping in a shallow flameproof dish. Sprinkle about 2 tablespoons of the sugar in an even layer over the bread and grill for about 2 minutes until the bread is toasted and the sugar is just starting to caramelise. Mix the cornflour into the fromage frais.

**2** Pile the fruit down the middle of the bread and sprinkle with 1 tablespoon of the sugar. Drop spoonfuls of the fromage-frais mixture on top, then sprinkle the rest of the sugar evenly over the top.

**3** Put the dish as close to the heat as you can and grill for about 6–8 minutes, until the fromage frais has browned and everything else is starting to bubble and turn juicy. Leave it to sit for a minute or two, then serve hot, spooned straight from the dish.

PER SERVING 211 kcals, protein 7g, carbs 47g, fat 1g, sat fat none, fibre 2g, sugar 22g, salt 0.45g

# Nutty caramel & choc sundaes

*Layers of chocolate and caramel sauces, ice cream and nuts – what could be simpler or more wickedly delicious?*

**TAKES 20 MINUTES, PLUS COOLING**
- **MAKES 6**

100g/4oz dark chocolate, broken into chunks
200ml/7fl oz milk
300g can caramel (we used Carnation)
85g/3oz crunchy peanut butter
4 crunchy biscuits, crumbled into chunks
50g/2oz salted roasted peanuts, chopped
6 big scoops vanilla ice cream
6 big scoops chocolate ice cream

**1** Put the chocolate and 100ml/3½fl oz of the milk in a small pan. Put the caramel, peanut butter and remaining milk in another pan. Gently melt both, stirring until saucy. Set aside to cool.

**2** Give the sauces a good stir to loosen, then layer the two sauces, biscuit bits, peanuts and ice cream in six sundae glasses or bowls, and eat straight away.

PER SUNDAE 608 kcals, protein 15g, carbs 62g, fat 34g, sat fat 15g, fibre 3g, sugar 55g, salt 0.8g

# Quick mango puddings

*The simplest dishes are often the most delicious, and this refreshing fruity pudding proves the point.*

**TAKES 5 MINUTES ● MAKES 6**

1 large ripe mango
6 scoops vanilla ice cream
2 tbsp thick cream
3 passion fruit

**1** Peel and dice the mango and whizz to a purée in a food processor.

**2** Add the scoops of vanilla ice cream and the thick cream to the food processor and whizz again. Spoon into six individual serving bowls. Halve the passion fruit, scoop out the flesh of each half and add to each bowl, then serve.

PER PUDDING 131 kcals, protein 2g, carbs 18g, fat 6g, sat fat 4g, fibre 2g, sugar 17g, salt 0.08g

# Cherry-chocolate meringue pots

*If you're serving this to children, use a good milk chocolate as they usually prefer it, or an orange-flavoured milk chocolate is also good. On the table in just under 15 minutes.*

**TAKES 15 MINUTES ● MAKES 4**

300ml pot double cream

4 shop-bought meringue nests, roughly broken

50g/2oz dark chocolate, broken into pieces

8 tbsp cherry compote (we used Bonne Maman)

shortbread fingers, to serve (optional)

**1** Whip the cream to soft peaks, then fold in the meringue pieces. Put the chocolate into a microwave-proof bowl and heat it in the microwave for 30–45 seconds or until melted, stirring halfway through.

**2** Spoon 2 tablespoons of the cherry compote into each of four glasses, then top with the meringue mix. Drizzle melted chocolate on top of each glass and serve with some shortbread fingers, if you like.

PER POT 504 kcals, protein 3g, carbs 27g, fat 44g, sat fat 25g, fibre 1g, sugar 26g, salt 0.08g

# Microwave coffee & walnut cake

*Coffee and walnuts are classic partners, and this quick pud can easily be put together from storecupboard staples. It's delicious served warm with custard.*

**TAKES 25 MINUTES • SERVES 4**

85g/3oz very soft butter
85g/3oz golden caster sugar
2 eggs, beaten
85g/3oz self-raising flour
2 tsp instant coffee powder
small handful walnut pieces

**FOR THE BUTTERCREAM**

1 tsp instant coffee powder
1 tsp milk
25g/1oz very soft butter
100g/4oz icing sugar

**1** In a medium bowl, beat the butter and sugar together until light and fluffy. Gradually add the eggs followed by the flour and instant coffee. Stir most of the walnuts into the batter, reserving a few for decoration. Transfer to a microwave-proof dish and cook on high for 2 minutes. Reduce the power to medium and cook for 2 minutes.

**2** After 4 minutes, check to see if the cake is cooked – it should be risen and spring back when touched. If it needs a bit longer, cook on medium for 1 minute more at a time, checking after each minute until the cake is cooked. Remove and allow to cool.

**3** Meanwhile, make the coffee buttercream. Dissolve the coffee in the milk, then add the butter and icing sugar. Beat until smooth, spread over the cake and top with the reserved walnuts.

PER SERVING 538 kcals, protein 7g, carbs 65g, fat 30g, sat fat 16g, fibre 1g, sugar 49g, salt 0.65g

# Chocolate & berry mousse pots

*Using chocolate with a high cocoa content means that you need less of it for a rich flavour. Use your own favourite mix of fruits for this surprisingly low-fat dessert.*

**TAKES 20 MINUTES** ● **MAKES 4**

75g/2½oz dark chocolate, grated
4 tbsp low-fat natural yogurt
2 egg whites
2 tsp caster sugar
350g/12oz berries (try blueberries, raspberries, cherries or a mix)

**1** Melt the chocolate in a heatproof bowl over a pan of simmering water, making sure the bowl doesn't directly touch the water. Once melted, allow it to cool for 5–10 minutes, then stir in the yogurt.

**2** Whisk the egg whites until stiff, then whisk in the sugar and beat until stiff again. Fold the whites into the chocolate mix – loosen the mixture first with a spoonful of egg white, then carefully fold in the rest, keeping as much air as possible.

**3** Put the berries into four small glasses or ramekins, then divide the chocolate mousse among them, spooning it on top of the fruit. Chill in the fridge until set.

PER POT 159 kcals, protein 5g, carbs 19g, fat 8g, sat fat 4g, fibre 3g, sugar 15g, salt 0.13g

# Nutty date & apricot pudding

*Medjool dates have a soft texture, with a wrinkled skin and sweet flesh. They break down into a delicious pulp when cooked, making them ideal for this moreish pud.*

**TAKES 20 MINUTES • SERVES 4**

6 Medjool dates, stoned and roughly chopped
handful chopped dried apricots
1 tsp ground mixed spice
2 tbsp clear honey
150ml/¼ pint orange juice
handful chopped mixed nuts
1 Madeira loaf cake
cream or ice cream, to serve

**1** Put the dates in a small pan with the apricots, spice and honey, then pour over the orange juice. Bring to the boil and cook for 5 minutes, until the dates have broken down and you have a thick, syrupy sauce. Stir in the nuts.

**2** Cut the cake in half lengthways, on the horizontal. Use a 150ml ramekin to cut out four circles from the cake. Divide the date mix among four ramekins, then top with the circles of cake, pressing them down gently. Cover with cling film and microwave on High for 3 minutes, then turn out on to a plate and serve with cream or ice cream.

PER SERVING 479 kcals, protein 7g, carbs 83g, fat 15g, sat fat 7g, fibre 4g, sugar 63g, salt 0.82g

# Griddled bananas with nutty chocolate custard

*An all-time children's favourite – chocolate, bananas and custard! If they're not nut lovers, sprinkle the puds with mini marshmallows or fudge pieces.*

**TAKES 15 MINUTES • SERVES 2**

2 ripe bananas
2 × 150g pots low-fat custard
4 squares dark chocolate
2 tbsp chopped toasted hazelnuts

**1** Heat a griddle pan until hot. Peel the bananas and slice them at an angle into 2cm/¾in slices. Cook the bananas on the griddle for 2–3 minutes each side until charred.

**2** Meanwhile, remove the lids from the custard pots and push 2 squares of the dark chocolate, chopped, into each one. Microwave each pot on high for 1 minute. Remove and leave to stand for 1 minute, then stir well.

**3** Divide the chocolate custard between two bowls, add the hot bananas and sprinkle each one with the chopped toasted hazelnuts.

PER SERVING 349 kcals, protein 8g, carbs 55g, fat 11g, sat fat 4g, fibre 2g, sugar 46g, salt 0.4g

# Honeyed almond figs

*When buying, look for plump figs, which should feel soft but not excessively so. They are best at room temperature, so take them out of the fridge an hour before serving.*

**TAKES 5 MINUTES ● SERVES 1**

2 ripe figs
2 tbsp 0% fat Greek yogurt
1 tbsp clear honey
pinch ground cinnamon
few flaked toasted almonds

**1** Cut the figs in half and arrange skin down on a plate.
**2** Spoon over the Greek yogurt, then drizzle with the honey. Sprinkle with a pinch of cinnamon and the flaked toasted almonds.

PER SERVING 151 kcals, protein 4g, carbs 24g, fat 5g, sat fat 1g, fibre 2g, sugar 11g, salt 0.07g

# Little iced lemon mousses

*You can make these ahead of time – just store in the fridge and transfer to the freezer roughly 1–1½ hours before you plan to eat them.*

**TAKES 10 MINUTES ● MAKES 6**

300g jar good-quality lemon curd
zest 1 lemon
300ml pot whipping or double cream
25g/1oz lemon shortbread or crunchy
    lemon-flavoured biscuits, plus extra
    to serve (optional)

**1** Put two-thirds of the lemon curd into a large bowl with the zest and cream, then beat with an electric whisk until it just holds its shape. Dribble over the rest of the lemon curd and divide among six small freezerproof glass pots, marbling the curd through as you go. Sit the pots on a small plate, cover the whole lot with cling film and freeze until ready to serve.

**2** Put the biscuits in a strong plastic bag and bash with the end of a rolling pin to crumbs. When you're ready to serve the pudding, remove the pots from the freezer (they should be ice cold but still soft and creamy), top with crumbs and serve with extra biscuits, if you like.

PER MOUSSE 354 kcals, protein 2g, carbs 35g, fat 24g, sat fat 13g, fibre none, sugar 23g, salt 0.14g

# Index

# Also available from BBC Books and *Good Food*